HRW

ALGEBRA ONE

INTERACTIONS

COURSE 1

LAB ACTIVITIES AND LONG-TERM PROJECTS

HOLT, RINEHART AND WINSTON
Harcourt Brace & Company
Austin • New York • Orlando • Atlanta • San Francisco • Boston • Dallas • Toronto • London

To the Teacher

Lab Activities and Long-Term Projects contains blackline masters that complement regular class-room use of *HRW Algebra One Interactions Course 1* and are especially helpful in accommodating students of varying interests, learning styles, and ability levels. There is one four-page Lab Activity and one four-page Long-Term Project for each chapter of *HRW Algebra One Interactions Course 1*.

- **Lab Activities** provide meaningful hands-on activities that facilitate concrete experiences of abstract mathematical concepts.
- **Long-Term Projects** engage students in activities that encompass more than one class period. Projects often require data collection or research to be done outside the classroom. Many of the projects are appropriate for group work.

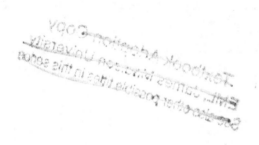
Developmental assistance by B&B Communications West, Inc.

HRW is a registered trademark licensed to Holt, Rinehart and Winston.

Printed in the United States of America

ISBN 0-03-051267-0

3   4   5   6   7   066   00   99   98

TABLE OF CONTENTS

Lab Activity
Factoring With Centimeter Cubes, Chapter 1

Materials
70 centimeter cubes

In this activity, you will use centimeter cubes to help you factor integers. If you do not have centimeter cubes, use sugar cubes, dice, or other cube-shaped blocks that are all the same size.

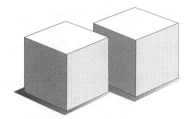

First review the factoring clues that you learned in Lesson 1.5. Match the numbers on the left with the divisibility rules on the right.

_____ **1.** 2   **a.** This number is a factor if both 2 and 3 are factors.

_____ **2.** 3   **b.** This number is a factor if the last digit is 0 or 5.

_____ **3.** 5   **c.** This number is a factor of all even numbers.

_____ **4.** 6   **d.** This number is a factor if the last digit is 0.

_____ **5.** 10   **e.** This number is a factor if it is a factor of the sum of the digits.

If you arrange a number of cubes into a rectangle, the length and width of the rectangle will be factors of the number of cubes that you used. Use this information to solve the following problems:

6. Arrange 6 cubes into a rectangle. What length and width did you use?

_____

7. Is there another way to arrange the 6 cubes into a rectangle? If so, how?

_____

8. Sketch your rectangles in the space below.

Lab Activity
Factoring With Centimeter Cubes, Chapter 1, page 2

9. Use your findings to make a list of the factors of 6. _____

10. Which of the factors are prime numbers? _____

11. What is the prime factorization of 6? _____

12. Arrange 20 cubes into a rectangle without using a width of 1 cm.

What length and width did you use? _____

13. Sketch your rectangle in the space below.

14. Which factor of 20 that you used for your rectangle is a composite

number? _____

15. Use this number of cubes to create another rectangle without using a

width of 1 cm. What length and width did you use? _____

16. Sketch your rectangle in the space below.

17. Write the prime factorization of 20.

_____

18. Rewrite the prime factorization in exponential form. _____

19. Use your cubes to construct a rectangular box with these prime
factorization numbers as the length, width, and height. Sketch your
box in the space below.

Lab Activity
Factoring With Centimeter Cubes, Chapter 1, page 3

20. Arrange 54 cubes into a rectangle without using a width of 1 cm. List the dimensions and sketch the rectangle in the space below.

21. One or both of your rectangle's dimensions are composite numbers. Use these composite numbers to create other rectangles. Sketch your rectangles in the space below, and label the length and width of each one.

22. What is the prime factorization of 54? _____

23. Rewrite the prime factorization in exponential form. _____

24. Explain why the prime factors of 54 cannot be used to create a rectangular box.

_____

_____

Use the same process and your centimeter cubes to determine the prime factorizations of the following numbers. Write the prime factorization in exponential form if possible.

25. 70 _____   **26.** 57 _____   **27.** 64 _____

_____

 Lab Activity
Factoring With Centimeter Cubes, Chapter 1, page 4

Use the same process and your pattern-recognition skills to determine the dimensions of the next rectangle in the sequence for finding the prime factors of each number. Write the prime factorization and sketch the next rectangle in the space provided.

28. 81 _____

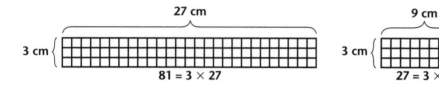

29. 120 _____

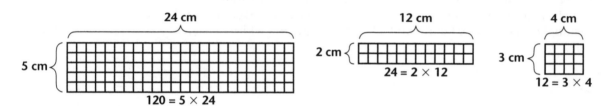

30. Choose a composite number. Create a pattern problem similar to Exercises 28 and 29.

Problem:

Answer:

Long-Term Project
Cleaning Up With Algebra, Chapter 1

In this project, you will use what you know about equations to solve problems. First read the Background Information that follows. It contains what you will need to formulate the equations and answer the questions.

Background Information

Phyllis owns a house-cleaning business in a large metropolitan area. She has opened a new office near a housing development that is being built. When it is finished, there will be 285 houses in the development. Phyllis normally offers her company's services at a rate of $75 per month.

To gain the business of more homeowners in the new development, she wants to use a promotional offer to encourage current customers to recruit new customers. She plans on giving a discount of $0.25 off the monthly rate for every customer after 100. For example, if there are 101 customers, the monthly rate for all customers would be $74.75 instead of $75; for 102 customers the rate would be $74.50 per month; for 103 customers the rate would be $74.25 per month, and so on. Phyllis needs to figure out how many customers will generate the most monthly income for her company.

1. How many customers do you estimate will generate the most monthly income for Phyllis's company? _____

2. Why might the company lose money after a certain number of

   customers? _____

3. If there are 100 or fewer customers, each customer pays $75 per month. Using i for income and c for the number of customers, write

   an equation for calculating the monthly income. _____

4. How much money would the company make per month if there are 32 customers? _____

5. How much money would the company make per month if there are 80 customers? _____

6. How much money would the company make per month if there are 100 customers? _____

7. If there are more than 100 customers, Phyllis uses the expression $(c - 100)(0.25)$. What does this expression represent?

   _____

   _____

Long-Term Project
Cleaning Up With Algebra, Chapter 1, page 2

8. How much money will each customer save if there are 105 customers? _____

9. How much money will each customer save if there are 172 customers? _____

10. Write an equation that can be used to calculate the price to charge each customer per month. Use d as the amount of the discount and p as the price per customer per month.

_____

11. If there are 105 customers, what is the price per customer per month? _____

12. If there are 117 customers, what is the price per customer per month? _____

13. If there are 128 customers, what is the price per customer per month? _____

14. Use the equations to complete the table on the following pages. Another option for completing the table is to create a spreadsheet.

$$d = (c - 100)(\$0.25) \qquad p = \$75 - d \qquad i = pc$$

15. How many customers are needed for the price to be less than $40 per

customer? _____

16. How much income is generated in one month by 150 customers? _____

by 250 customers? _____

17. How many customers does Phyllis need in order to generate the

maximum amount of monthly income with this promotional deal? _____

18. How does the answer compare with your estimate?

_____

19. Write an equation for calculating yearly income, using the same

variables as for monthly income and y as yearly income. _____

20. If there are 127 customers, what would the company's yearly income be? _____

21. What is the maximum amount of income that Phyllis can generate

in one year? _____

22. Do you think that Phyllis's discount promotion is a good idea? Why or why not?

_____

_____

Long-Term Project
Cleaning Up With Algebra, Chapter 1, page 3

c	d	p	i		c	d	p	i
100					147			
101					148			
102					149			
103					150			
104					151			
105					152			
106					153			
107					154			
108					155			
109					156			
110					157			
111					158			
112					159			
113					160			
114					161			
115					162			
116					163			
117					164			
118					165			
119					166			
120					167			
121					168			
122					169			
123					170			
124					171			
125					172			
126					173			
127					174			
128					175			
129					176			
130					177			
131					178			
132					179			
133					180			
134					181			
135					182			
136					183			
137					184			
138					185			
139					186			
140					187			
141					188			
142					189			
143					190			
144					191			
145					192			
146					193			

Long-Term Project
Cleaning Up With Algebra, Chapter 1, page 4

c	d	p	i
194			
195			
196			
197			
198			
199			
200			
201			
202			
203			
204			
205			
206			
207			
208			
209			
210			
211			
212			
213			
214			
215			
216			
217			
218			
219			
220			
221			
222			
223			
224			
225			
226			
227			
228			
229			
230			
231			
232			
233			
234			
235			
236			
237			
238			
239			
240			

c	d	p	i
241			
242			
243			
244			
245			
246			
247			
248			
249			
250			
251			
252			
253			
254			
255			
256			
257			
258			
259			
260			
261			
262			
263			
264			
265			
266			
267			
268			
269			
270			
271			
272			
273			
274			
275			
276			
277			
278			
279			
280			
281			
282			
283			
284			
285			

Lab Activity
Working With Integers, Chapter 2

Materials
40 counters, 20 each of two different colors
colored pencils that match the counters
ruler
paper

First decide on one color to represent positive numbers and the other color to represent negative numbers. Record your color assignments:

positive = _____   negative = _____

Use the counters to model the following problems, in which you combine positive and negative integers. Remember that one positive counter paired with one negative counter is equal to zero and is called a neutral pair. After you have made as many neutral pairs as you can, the remaining counters represent the solution.

1. $-13 + 8 =$ _____   Sketch your counters and circle any neutral pairs that you make.

2. $9 + (-2) =$ _____   Sketch your counters and circle any neutral pairs that you make.

Lab Activity
Working With Integers, Chapter 2, page 2

3. $-21 + 17 =$ _____

Sketch your counters and circle any neutral pairs that you make.

4. $-7 + 10 + (-3) + 5 =$ _____

Sketch your counters and circle any neutral pairs that you make.

5. Write some guidelines that will help you to remember what to do when combining positive and negative integers.

_____

_____

_____

Use your guidelines to solve the following problems:

6. $754 + (-322) =$ _____   **7.** $-118 + 267 =$ _____

8. $1249 + 231 =$ _____   **9.** $-2005 + 894 =$ _____

10. $-236 + (-67) + 975 + (-532) =$ _____   **11.** $-12 + 32 + 401 + (-1120) =$ _____

12. $-802 + 581 + 802 + (-587) =$ _____

13. $1361 + (-1007) + (-28) + (-306) =$ _____

Lab Activity
Working With Integers, Chapter 2, page 3

14. You learned in the opener to Chapter 2 that the highest known land elevation is the top of Mount Everest, which is 29,028 feet above sea level. The lowest known dry land is in the Dead Sea, which has an elevation of −1312 feet. What is the difference in elevation between these two points?

_____

15. In the United States, the highest point is the peak of Mount McKinley in Alaska at an elevation of 20,320 feet. The lowest point of dry land in the United States is in Death Valley, California, at an elevation of −282 feet. What is the difference between the lowest point and the highest point in the United States?

_____

Construct a number line diagonally on a separate piece of paper. Make it 12 inches long with numbers spaced one-half of an inch apart. Place one of your counters at a point near the middle of the number line and label that point 0. Move your counter along the number line to solve the following problems. A move to the right is positive and a move to the left is negative. The final stopping point is your answer.

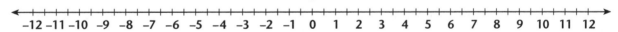

16. −7 + 9 = _____   Sketch your movement on the number line:

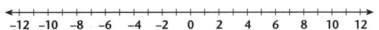

17. 4 + (−11) = _____   Sketch your movement on the number line:

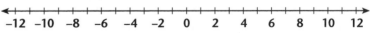

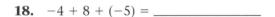

Lab Activity
Working With Integers, Chapter 2, page 4

18. −4 + 8 + (−5) = _____   Sketch your movement on the number line:

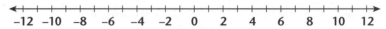

19. −10 + 18 + (−3) + (−5) = _____   Sketch your movement on the number line:

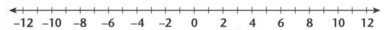

Accountants and bankers use the concepts of positive and negative numbers all the time. After all transactions have taken place, an account is considered "in the red" if the balance is negative and "in the black" if the balance is positive. Owing money to someone else is represented by a negative number. Use these ideas to evaluate the following account:

20. Miles has an account at First City Bank. At the beginning of the week his account balance was $1276.78. During the week he made the following transactions:

  Check written to "The Gas Corner" for $23.88
  Cash withdrawal from the ATM machine for $40.00
  Paycheck deposit of $576.34
  Check written to "Pizza Guy" for $17.65
  Check written to Mr. Landlord for $750.00

What is his balance at the end of the week? _____

Is he "in the red" or "in the black"? _____

21. Write an original problem of your own that uses the concepts of positive and negative numbers. Be sure to include the answer to your problem.

_____

_____

_____

_____

_____

_____

Long-Term Project
Planning a Vacation, Chapter 2

Todd and Eric have decided to take a spring-break vacation. They are both college students with a limited amount of money, so they are trying to plan an inexpensive trip. They are going to school in Colorado and would like to go somewhere warm for their trip. Todd would like to go to Florida, and Eric would like to go to California. They have agreed to go to whichever destination will be cheaper. In this project, you will help them calculate the most inexpensive choice for their trip.

The first thing Todd and Eric must research is how to get to their destination. The only options they have decided to consider are flying or driving. The table shows the rates they were quoted for flying.

Destination	Airline Ticket Price*
Florida	$272.00
California	$203.00

*round-trip price per person

Since only Eric owns a car and his car is old and unreliable, they will need to rent a car if they drive. If they drive, they will need a car for a total of 9 days. Todd called a few rental-car companies and received the rental rate information shown below. The car must be picked up and dropped off at the same rental location for these rates to apply.

Mr. Car Rentals:	$19.95 per day plus $0.19 per mile $39.99 per day unlimited miles $248.79 per week unlimited miles
Cross-Country Cars:	$21.50 per day plus $0.17 per mile $41.50 per day unlimited miles $225.50 per week unlimited miles
Attractive Auto Rental:	$14.95 per day plus $0.15 per mile no unlimited miles or weekly rates

Using an atlas or other map, determine the number of miles for the two possible trips.

1. Denver to Daytona Beach—round trip

2. Denver to San Diego—round trip

_____

_____

Long-Term Project
Planning a Vacation, Chapter 2, page 2

Write an equation for each of the car-rental companies that can be used to calculate the cost of a rental car at the daily rate with a charge per mile. Use *t* as the total cost, *d* as the number of days, and *m* as the number of miles.

3. Mr. Car Rentals: _____

4. Cross-Country Cars: _____

5. Attractive Auto Rental: _____

Write an equation for each of the car-rental companies that can be used to calculate the cost of a rental car at the daily rate with unlimited miles. Use *t* as the total cost and *d* as the number of days.

6. Mr. Car Rentals: _____

7. Cross-Country Cars: _____

8. Attractive Auto Rental: _____

Write an equation for each of the car-rental companies that can be used to calculate the cost of a rental car for one week at the weekly rate plus the extra days at the daily rate with a charge per mile. Use *t* as the total cost, *d* as the number of days, and *m* as the number of miles.

9. Mr. Car Rentals: _____

10. Cross-Country Cars: _____

11. Attractive Auto Rental: _____

Write an equation for each of the car-rental companies that can be used to calculate the cost of a rental car at the weekly rate for one week plus the extra days at the daily rate with unlimited miles. Use *t* as the total cost and *d* as the number of days.

12. Mr. Car Rentals: _____

13. Cross-Country Cars: _____

14. Attractive Auto Rental: _____

Long-Term Project
Planning a Vacation, Chapter 2, page 3

15. Fill in the table by using your equations to calculate the total costs. Todd and Eric estimate that in addition to the number of miles they will drive to get to their vacation site, they will drive no more than 200 additional miles at their vacation site. You can use the one-way distance to the vacation destination as the number of miles they will drive during the last two days.

		Florida	California
Mr. Car Rentals	daily rate with a charge per mile daily rate with unlimited miles weekly rate plus daily rate with a charge per mile weekly rate plus daily rate with unlimited miles		
Cross-Country Cars	daily rate with a charge per mile daily rate with unlimited miles weekly rate plus daily rate with a charge per mile weekly rate plus daily rate with unlimited miles		
Attractive Auto Rental	daily rate with a charge per mile daily rate with unlimited miles weekly rate plus daily rate with a charge per mile weekly rate plus daily rate with unlimited miles		

16. What is the cheapest car-rental option for driving to Daytona Beach,

Florida? _____

17. What is the cheapest car-rental option for driving to San Diego,

California? _____

If they decide to fly, they would like to rent a car at the airport upon arrival. Assume that the car-rental rates at the airports are the same as the rates given on the first page. They estimate that they will not need to drive more than 200 total miles while on their vacation, but they will need to keep the car for the same number of days because they cannot return it to the airport until the day of the return flight. Assume that they drive a total of 50 miles the last two days.

Write equations for the total cost of flying and renting a car for each car rental company at each rental rate. Use t as total cost, a as the airline ticket price, d as the number of days, and m as the number of miles.

18. Mr. Car Rentals:
   a. daily rate with a charge per mile: _____

   b. daily rate with unlimited miles: _____

   c. weekly rate plus daily rate with a charge per mile: _____

   d. weekly rate plus daily rate with unlimited miles: _____

Long-Term Project
Planning a Vacation, Chapter 2, page 4

19. Cross-Country Cars:

    a. daily rate with a charge per mile: _____

    b. daily rate with unlimited miles: _____

    c. weekly rate plus daily rate with a charge per mile: _____

    d. weekly rate plus daily rate with unlimited miles: _____

20. Attractive Auto Rental:

    a. daily rate with a charge per mile: _____

    b. daily rate with unlimited miles: _____

    c. weekly rate plus daily rate with a charge per mile: _____

    d. weekly rate plus daily rate with unlimited miles: _____

21. Use your equations to calculate the total cost to fly and rent a car, and fill in the table.

		Florida	California
Mr. Car Rentals	daily rate with a charge per mile daily rate with unlimited miles weekly rate plus daily rate with a charge per mile weekly rate plus daily rate with unlimited miles		
Cross Country Cars	daily rate with a charge per mile daily rate with unlimited miles weekly rate plus daily rate with a charge per mile weekly rate plus daily rate with unlimited miles		
Attractive Auto Rental	daily rate with a charge per mile daily rate with unlimited miles weekly rate plus daily rate with a charge per mile weekly rate plus daily rate with unlimited miles		

22. What is the cheapest option for flying and renting a car in Daytona

Beach, Florida? _____

23. What is the cheapest option for flying and renting a car in San Diego,

California? _____

24. What factors may have been overlooked in the cost comparisons?

_____

25. Which of the vacation options is the cheapest for Todd and Eric? Explain.

_____

 Lab Activity
How Many Beans? Chapter 3

Materials
small plastic bag containing multicolored jelly beans or small multicolored buttons

In this lab you will use different colors of jelly beans to help you learn about fractions, ratios, proportions, percents, probabilities, and decimals.

1. Pour out the jelly beans, and separate them into piles by color. Write the colors and the number of jelly beans of each color in the space provided.

2. What is the total number of jelly beans in your bag? _____

3. Write fractions for each color to represent the portion of the total number. Use the number of jelly beans of one color as the numerator and the total number of jelly beans as the denominator. Reduce your fractions to simplest form.

4. Which color makes up closest to $\frac{1}{4}$ of the total amount? _____

5. Which color makes up closest to $\frac{1}{2}$ of the total amount? _____

Lab Activity
How Many Beans? Chapter 3, page 2

6. In the space provided, write the colors and their fractions in order from least to greatest.

7. Write each list of fractions as decimals by dividing the numerator by the denominator. List the colors and their decimals in the space provided.

8. What is the sum of the fractions you listed for Exercise 6? _____

9. In your own words, explain why that sum makes sense. _____

_____

10. What is the fractional sum of the red and yellow jelly beans? _____

11. What is the difference between the fraction for the color with the

largest number and the fraction for the color with the smallest number? _____

12. Find one-half of the fraction that represents the green jelly beans. _____

The fractions you calculated for each color of jelly beans can also be thought of as ratios. For example, if there are 12 red jelly beans out of a total of 48, then the ratio of red jelly beans to the total number of jelly beans would be 12:48, or 1:4 in simplest form. Use your fractions as ratios to answer the next set of questions.

 **Lab Activity**
How Many Beans? Chapter 3, page 3

13. Rewrite your fractions as ratios in the following form:
number of one color : total number

_____

14. Using your ratios, how many green jelly beans would there be in a bag

of 250 jelly beans? _____

15. How many yellow jelly beans would there be in a bag of 400 jelly beans? _____

16. What is the ratio of jelly beans that are not red, blue, or yellow to the

total number of jelly beans in your bag? _____

17. Write a problem in which you must use your color ratios to calculate
the number of jelly beans of a certain color in a bag of jelly beans. Be
sure to provide the answer.

_____

_____

18. If you wanted to share your jelly beans with two other people so that
each of you received the same color ratios, how many of each color
would each person receive? (You may need to cut the jelly beans into
pieces.)

_____

19. Calculate the percent of each color that was in your bag of jelly beans.
List the colors and their percents in the space provided.

20. What is the sum of the percents you listed in Exercise 19? _____

21. In your own words, explain why that sum makes sense.

_____

22. If you gave away 10 of your jelly beans to a friend, what percent

would you be giving away? _____

Lab Activity
How Many Beans? Chapter 3, page 4

23. What percent of your jelly beans are red, blue, or yellow? _____

24. If you ate $\frac{1}{2}$ of the green jelly beans and $\frac{1}{3}$ of the red jelly beans, what

percent of the total would you have eaten? _____

Your fractions from Exercise 6 can also be thought of as probabilities.
Use your fractions as probabilities to answer the next set of questions.

25. Suppose that you placed all the jelly beans back into the bag and
shook the bag to mix them up. If you reached into the bag and took
out a jelly bean without looking, what is the probability that the jelly
bean would be yellow?

_____

26. If you replaced that jelly bean and picked another one, what is the
probability that it would be some color other than red?

_____

27. If you chose a green jelly bean and did not replace it, what is the
probability that the next one you chose would be red?

_____

28. Using your color fractions, write a probability problem of your own.
Be sure to include the answer to your problem.

_____

_____

29. Describe another type of situation in which you might use fractions,
ratios, proportions, percents, probabilities, and decimals. Be sure to
explain how each form might be used.

_____

_____

_____

_____

Long-Term Project
Traffic Timing, Chapter 3

Suppose that you are a traffic-light timing expert for a medium-sized city with an increasing population. More people means more drivers, which means more traffic-control devices. Use what you learned about fractions, percents, ratios, proportions, probabilities, and decimals to solve these problems involving the timing of traffic lights.

A light on Washington Street is currently set at 3 minutes for green, 1 minute for yellow, and 2 minutes for red for each cycle. Write the fractions for the amount of time that the light spends on each color during one cycle. Be sure to write them in simplest form.

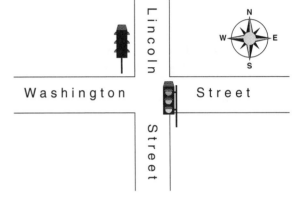

1. green _____

2. yellow _____

3. red _____

The light at the same intersection on Lincoln Street is green for $1\frac{1}{2}$ minutes, yellow for $\frac{1}{2}$ minute, and red for 4 minutes. Write the fractions

for the amount of time in minutes that the light spends on each color for one cycle. Be sure to write them in simplest form.

4. green _____   **5.** yellow _____   **6.** red _____

On Sunday through Thursday, the traffic lights at this intersection operate from 5:00 A.M. until 10 P.M. The remainder of the time, the lights flash yellow in one direction and red in the other direction. Based on the timing ratios you calculated above, calculate the number of minutes that the lights are each color on a Monday. Remember to consider only the amount of time the lights are operating normally, not flashing.

7. Washington Street: green = _____   yellow = _____   red = _____

8. Lincoln Street: green = _____   yellow = _____   red = _____

Long-Term Project
Traffic Timing, Chapter 3, page 2

On Friday and Saturday, the same traffic lights operate on the same cycle from 5:00 A.M. until midnight. Calculate the number of minutes that the lights are each color on a Friday.

9. Washington Street: green = _____ yellow = _____ red = _____

10. Lincoln Street: green = _____ yellow = _____ red = _____

Calculate the amount of time in hours that the lights spend on each color for one week: Sunday at 5:00 A.M. to Saturday at midnight. Give your answer in hours and fractions of hours, not in hours and minutes.

11. Washington Street: green = _____ yellow = _____ red = _____

12. Lincoln Street: green = _____ yellow = _____ red = _____

Write the ratios for the colors of the traffic lights in terms of

$$\frac{\text{number of hours on each color in one week}}{\text{number of hours operating normally (not flashing) in one week}}.$$

13. Washington Street: green _____ yellow _____ red _____

14. Lincoln Street: green _____ yellow _____ red _____

Convert these ratios to percents.

15. Washington Street: green _____ yellow _____ red _____

16. Lincoln Street: green _____ yellow _____ red _____

This intersection is becoming busier, and the traffic-light timing needs to be altered. If the times for one cycle are altered as listed below, write the fractions for the amount of time in seconds that the light spends on each color for one cycle. Be sure to write the fractions in simplest form.

Washington Street: green = 5 minutes   yellow = 1.5 minutes   red = 3 minutes

Lincoln Street: green = 2 minutes   yellow = 1 minute   red = 6.5 minutes

17. Washington Street: green = _____ yellow = _____ red = _____

18. Lincoln Street: green = _____ yellow = _____ red = _____

Long-Term Project
Traffic Timing, Chapter 3, page 3

19. The manager of the Department of Transportation and the police chief have recommended that the intersection receive left-turn arrows on Washington Street because of the number of accidents at the intersection. You decide to solve the problem by adding left-turn arrows on Washington Street and having them green for $\frac{1}{5}$ of the time allotted for the green light. Adjust your ratios for Washington Street to account for this addition.

green left-turn arrow _____   green _____

yellow _____   red _____

20. What is the probability that a person driving up to the intersection on

Lincoln Street will have a green light? _____

21. What is the probability that a person driving up to the intersection on

Washington Street will have the green left-turn arrow? _____

After meeting with the city planner, you know that in the future this intersection will be expanded by increasing the number of lanes to accommodate the increase in traffic resulting from the construction of nearby shopping areas and houses. You predict the following conditions:

- Washington Street will have two left-turn lanes in each direction that require green, yellow, and red left-turn arrows.

- Lincoln Street will have one left-turn lane in each direction that requires green, yellow, and red left-turn arrows.

- Washington Street traffic will be heavier than Lincoln Street traffic.

- The intersection will be heavily traveled and will need short cycle times to keep the cars moving fairly quickly.

22. Given these conditions, develop a plan for how much time each light should be on in each direction on each street. Remember that when the light is green or yellow on one street, the light must be red on the other street.

_____

_____

_____

Long-Term Project
Traffic Timing, Chapter 3, page 4

Write the timing ratios in seconds for each light, based on the plan you developed for Exercise 22.

23. Washington Street:

green left-turn arrow _____   green light _____

yellow left-turn arrow _____   yellow light _____

red left-turn arrow _____   red light _____

24. Lincoln Street:

green left-turn arrow _____   green light _____

yellow left-turn arrow _____   yellow light _____

red left-turn arrow _____   red light _____

25. Based on your plan, what is the probability that a person driving up to the intersection on Lincoln Street will have a red light? _____

26. What is the probability that a person driving up to the intersection on Washington Street will have a yellow left-turn arrow? _____

27. How many minutes during rush hour each evening will Washington Street's lights be green (not including the left-turn arrow) if rush hour is from 4:00 P.M. to 6:00 P.M.? _____

28. To access the shopping areas, a car must turn left from Washington Street to go south on Lincoln Street, turn right to go south on Lincoln Street from Washington Street, or continue south on Lincoln Street. The future shop owners would like to know how many minutes per hour the lights will be green to allow the cars turning left and the cars continuing south to come to their stores. _____

29. A rush-hour traffic jam can create conditions in which each car requires 10 seconds to get through an intersection during a green light. Using your plan for the future intersection traffic-light timing, how many cars could get through the intersection in one light cycle? _____

30. If these conditions lasted for 45 minutes, how many cars could get through the intersection? _____

31. Do you think your plan will be acceptable? Why or why not?

_____

_____

Lab Activity
The Shape of Things, Chapter 4

Materials
construction paper
scissors
protractor
ruler

In this activity, you will be constructing different polygons and creating
problems with them.

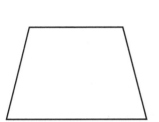 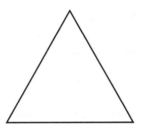  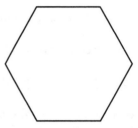

1. What are the measures of the angles of a square? _____

   Using your construction paper, pencil, protractor, and scissors,
   construct a square with 2-inch sides.

2. What are the measures of the angles of an equilateral triangle?_____

   Construct an equilateral triangle with 2-inch sides.

3. What are the measures of the angles of an isosceles triangle if one of

   the base angles is 30°?_____

   Construct an isosceles triangle with these angle measurements and a
   2-inch base.

4. What are the measures of the base angles of an isosceles right triangle? _____

   Construct an isosceles right triangle with a hypotenuse of 2 inches.

5. What are the measures of the interior angles of a regular pentagon? _____

   Construct a regular pentagon with sides of 2 inches.

6. What does it mean if a pentagon is irregular? _____

   _____

   Construct an irregular convex pentagon whose longest side is 2 inches.

Lab Activity
The Shape of Things, Chapter 4, page 2

7. What are the measures of the second pair of opposite angles in a

rhombus if the first pair of opposite angles are 60° each? _____

Construct a rhombus with these angle measurements and sides of
2 inches.

8. What is a quadrilateral? _____

Construct a quadrilateral whose longest side is 2 inches.

9. If an isosceles trapezoid has base angles of 30°, what are the measures

of the other two angles? _____

Construct an isosceles trapezoid with these angle measurements and
whose longest base is 2 inches.

10. What are the measures of the interior angles of a regular hexagon?_____

Construct a regular hexagon with 2-inch sides.

**For the next two questions, have the polygons you constructed
on the table or desk in front of you.**

11. Without measuring, which of your polygons has the greatest perimeter?
How do you know?

_____

_____

_____

_____

12. Without measuring, which of your polygons have the same perimeter?
How do you know?

_____

_____

_____

_____

 **Lab Activity**
The Shape of Things, Chapter 4, page 3

For the next set of questions, you will be asked to identify a polygon or group of polygons from a set of clues. You may want to have your polygons in front of you as you determine the answers.

Which of the polygons fit the clues? Explain your reasoning.

13. The polygon is convex.
    All of its sides are congruent.
    The polygon has at least one obtuse angle.

    _____

14. The polygon is convex.
    It is regular.
    The polygon has all acute angles.

    _____

15. It is a convex polygon.
    The polygon has at least one right angle.
    There are at least two congruent sides.

    _____

16. It is a convex polygon.
    It is isosceles.
    It is not a quadrilateral.

    _____

17. The polygon is convex.
    The polygon is a quadrilateral.
    It has exactly two different angle measurements.

    _____

18. It is a convex polygon.
    It has at least one right angle.
    The perimeter of the polygon is 8 inches.

    _____

19. The polygon is convex.
    It is irregular.
    It has more than three sides.

    _____

Lab Activity
The Shape of Things, Chapter 4, page 4

For the next set of exercises, you will create lists of clues based on your knowledge of polygons. You may want to have your polygons in front of you as you determine the answers.

20. Create a list of clues that will fit only one of your polygons. Include the answer.

_____

_____

21. Create a list of clues that will fit exactly two of your polygons. Include the answer.

_____

_____

22. Create a list of clues that will fit more than two of your polygons. Include the answer.

_____

_____

23. Create a list of clues that will fit all of your polygons. Include the answer.

_____

_____

24. Create a list of clues that will fit any number of your polygons. Include the answer.

_____

_____

25. Create a list of clues that describes a polygon but will not fit any of your polygons.

_____

_____

26. What kind of polygon does the list of clues you wrote for Exercise 25 describe?_____

_____

_____

Long-Term Project
Designing With Lines and Angles, Chapter 4

Use what you learned about lines, angles, triangles, and other polygons to create a design and describe it mathematically. You will need a ruler, a protractor, a pencil, and some scratch paper or graph paper to complete this project.

Before you begin, write a definition in your own words for each of the following terms. Draw a diagram to illustrate each term when appropriate.

1. acute angle _____

2. right angle _____

3. obtuse angle _____

4. complementary angles _____

5. supplementary angles _____

6. parallel lines _____

7. perpendicular lines _____

8. transversal _____

9. scale factor _____

10. concave polygon _____

11. convex polygon _____

12. isosceles triangle _____

13. equilateral triangle _____

14. scalene triangle _____

15. regular polygon _____

16. Choose an item for which you will draw a diagram or design. It could be a room in a house, an artistic design, a computer desk, the outside of a building, a section of a bridge, a piece of playground equipment, or anything that uses straight lines and angles in its design. Your item should be something that could not be drawn life-size on a piece of notebook or graph paper. List or describe your item here.

_____

_____

Long-Term Project
Designing With Lines and Angles, Chapter 4, page 2

17. Choose a scale factor to use for the drawing of your item. Use a factor that will be easy to convert and apply given your tools and paper size. Record your scale factor here.

_____

18. Use your ruler and protractor to draw the item as accurately as possible. Take actual measurements whenever possible. Estimate other measurements, if necessary. You may need to spend some time with a tape measure and the actual item to get the actual measurements. Or you could research the measurements, such as the actual height of one story of a building, and use your research to estimate the measurements of your item. You may also want to use graph paper to help you draw your items more easily.

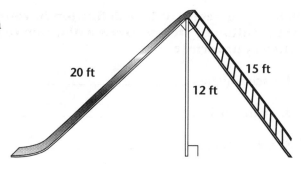

19. Mark angle measurements and other measurements on your drawing. Make note of any parallel lines, perpendicular lines, and transversals.

20. Now describe the item you drew in mathematical terms. Write your description as a series of construction steps so that someone who is not looking at your drawing could duplicate it by following the steps. Be sure to use the terms you defined at the beginning of this project in your description. Try to use each term at least once in your construction steps. Also use specific measurements of line segments and angles so that your steps are as accurate as possible. Use the space on the next page to write your steps.

Long-Term Project
Designing With Lines and Angles, Chapter 4, page 3

Item _____

Scale factor _____

_____

_____

_____

_____

_____

_____

_____

_____

_____

_____

_____

_____

_____

_____

_____

_____

_____

_____

_____

_____

_____

_____

Long-Term Project
Designing With Lines and Angles, Chapter 4, page 4

21. After you have completed your description in the form of construction steps, read through them to make sure that your steps can be followed to create your drawing.

22. Exchange construction steps with another student in your class. You may tell him or her what the item is, but DO NOT show your drawing to him or her.

23. Read the other student's description, and draw the item according to the construction steps that he or she has created. Include as much detail as possible.

After both of you have finished creating a drawing from the construction steps, exchange drawings again and check each other's work. Answer the following questions:

24. Did your partner's sketch match your sketch? _____

25. In what ways did your sketches differ? _____

_____

26. If there were mistakes, were they caused by problems with the construction steps? What revisions would you make to your construction steps to make them easier to follow and more accurate? (You may want to consult with the student who followed your steps to answer this question.)

_____

_____

27. What problems did you encounter while trying to follow your partner's construction steps?

_____

28. What revisions to your partner's steps would be helpful to someone else who is trying to duplicate the drawing? (Share these ideas with that student.)

_____

29. Did the use of mathematical terminology improve your ability to describe your drawing? Why or why not?

_____

Lab Activity
Concentration—Algebra-Style, Chapter 5

Materials
game board and cover squares
scissors

In this game of Concentration, you will match algebraic expressions with equivalent expressions in a simplified form. To make your game board, follow these steps:

Step 1 Copy and cut out the game board on page 2.

Step 2 Copy and cut out each of the squares numbered from 1 to 24 on page 2.

Step 3 Starting at the top left-hand corner, cover each square on the game board in sequence with one of the numbered squares you cut out.

Twelve of the squares on the game board contain algebraic expressions involving addition and/or subtraction. The other 12 squares contain the results in simplified form. The object of the game is to match each algebraic expression with its simplified form.

You can play the game alone or with a partner. Randomly pick one square, and remove the numbered square covering it. Then randomly pick a second square, and remove the numbered square. If the expressions match, you win one point and go again. If they do not match, recover the squares. Then the next player tries to make a match.

Use one of the score cards on page 3 to keep score. When a match is made and a point is scored, write the expression and its equivalent on the score card. When all the squares are uncovered, the player with the most points is the winner.

1. Play the game with a partner. As you play, try to understand the relationship between the expressions and their sum or difference in simplified form.

2. Cut out the blank game board on page 4. Make up your own game board containing 12 algebraic expressions and their simplified form. Play the game with a partner, and keep score.

Lab Activity
Concentration—Algebra-Style, Chapter 5, page 2

$-(x + y)$	$-x + y - y$	$2x - (-1)$ $- 2x$	$(x + y) -$ $(y + x)$	$-x - y$	$x - (x + 1)$
$2x + y$ $- x - y$	$x + y - 2x$	-1	$-x + y$	$-x$	$(x + 1) -$ $(x - 1)$
x	$2(x + y) -$ $(x + y)$	$x + (y - x)$	y	$x + y$	2
1	$2x - 3y$ $-x + 2y$	$x - y$	0	$x - (x + y)$	$-y$

1	2	3	4	5	6
7	8	9	10	11	12
13	14	15	16	17	18
19	20	21	22	23	24

 **Lab Activity**
Concentration—Algebra-Style, Chapter 5, page 3

SCORE CARD

Player 1 _____

Player 2 _____

SCORE CARD

Player 1 _____

Player 2 _____

Lab Activity
Concentration—Algebra-Style, Chapter 5, page 4

Use the space provided and make up your own game involving algebraic expressions. Describe the game and write the rules. Sketch any game boards or playing pieces needed to play the game.

_____

_____

_____

_____

_____

_____

_____

_____

_____

_____

Long-Term Project
Algebraic Magic Squares, Chapter 5

A **magic square** is a square array of numbers arranged so that the sum of each row, column, and main diagonal is equal to the same "magic-square" constant. In this project, you will investigate some properties of magic squares and construct magic squares by using algebraic expressions. Then you will learn another way to arrange algebraic expressions so that they have "magical" properties.

1. Add the numbers in each row, column, and diagonal of this square array of numbers. How are the sums related?

1	8	10	15
12	13	3	6
7	2	16	9
14	11	5	4

_____

_____

2. This array has six *broken diagonals*: (8, 3, 9, 14); (10, 6, 7, 11); (10, 13, 7, 4); (8, 12, 9, 5); (12, 2, 5, 15); and (6, 16, 11, 1). Find the sum of the numbers in each broken diagonal. How are the sums related?

_____

_____

3. A magic square is said to be *panmagic* if the sum of each broken diagonal is also equal to the magic-square constant. Is the square array in Exercise 1 a panmagic square? Explain.

_____

_____

4. Rotate the square array from Exercise 1 counterclockwise 90° by filling in this square array. Describe any "magical" qualities of the new square array.

14			1
4			15

_____

_____

5. Now reflect the square array from Exercise 4 about the vertical axis by filling in this square array. Describe any "magical" qualities of this square array.

1			14
15			4

_____

_____

Long-Term Project
Algebraic Magic Squares, Chapter 5, page 2

6. Solve each of the following problems. Write your answer in the corresponding square of the array.

a. $x - 10 = 10$

b. $x + 4 = 12$

c. $x - 32 = -21$

d. $(-15) + x = 8$

e. $4 = x - 11$

f. $14 = -(5 - x)$

g. $6\frac{3}{4} - x = -9\frac{1}{4}$

h. $10 = x - 2$

i. $k - 7 = 10$

j. $x - 2.3 = 10.7$

k. $y - 12.5 = 1.5$

l. Find the cost of a roast weighing 7.2 pounds if the price per pound is $2.50.

$\overline{a}$	$\overline{b}$	$\overline{c}$	$\overline{d}$
$\overline{e}$	$\overline{f}$	$\overline{g}$	$\overline{h}$
$\overline{i}$	$\overline{j}$	$\overline{k}$	$\overline{l}$
$\overline{m}$	$\overline{n}$	$\overline{o}$	$\overline{p}$

m. The product of 2 and a number is 20. Find the number.

n. Two angles of a triangle each measure 79°. Find the measure of the third angle.

o. A number decreased by 7 is 14. Find the number.

p. The range of a set of scores is 9. If the highest score is 18, what is the lowest score?

7. Is the array a magic square? Is it a panmagic square? Explain.

_____

_____

Long-Term Project
Algebraic Magic Squares, Chapter 5, page 3

8. Add the expressions in each row, column, and main diagonal of the array. Describe the sums.

_____

$x - 7$	$x - 6$	$x - 1$	$x + 4$
$x - 2$	$x + 5$	$x - 8$	$x - 5$
$x - 4$	$x - 9$	$x + 2$	$x + 1$
$x + 3$	x	$x - 3$	$x - 10$

9. List the elements in the six broken diagonals of this array.

_____

10. Find the sum of each broken diagonal.

_____

11. Explain why the array is a panmagic square.

_____

12. Complete this square array so that it will be a magic square.

$x - 7$			
		$x - 5$	
			$x + 3$
$x + 2$			$x - 2$

13. Add 3 to each expression of the magic square. Is the new square magic? Is it panmagic? Explain.

_____

14. Subtract 4 from each expression of the magic square in Exercise 12. Is the new square magic? Is it panmagic? Explain.

_____

Long-Term Project

Algebraic Magic Squares, Chapter 5, page 4

Magic squares can also be arranged in a planetarium array.

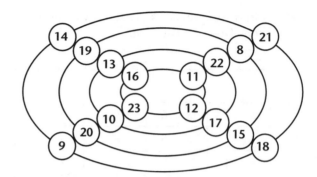

15. Add the numbers on each of the four concentric ellipses, and on each of the four aligned orbital paths. Describe the sums.

_____

_____

16. Complete this planetarium array so that the magic-square constant is 62.

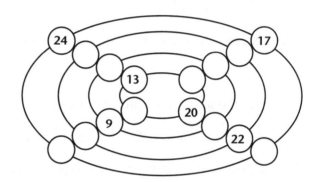

17. Subtract 10 from each number in the array from Exercise 16. Is the new array a planetarium array?

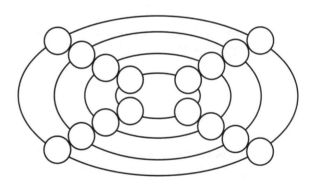

18. Complete this planetarium array so that the magic-square constant is $4x + 6$.

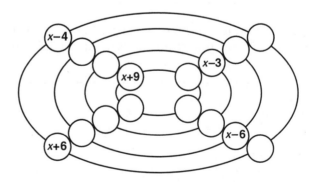

Lab Activity
Equation Wheel, Chapter 6

Materials
equation wheel and viewer templates
scissors
toothpick

In this activity you will construct an equation wheel to give you practice in writing multiplication and division equations and applying the correct property to solve them. To make your equation wheel, follow these steps:

Step 1 Copy and cut out the equation viewer on page 3. Then cut out the slots indicated with dashed lines to make the viewing windows.

Step 2 Place the viewer directly over the equation wheel on page 4. Insert the point of a toothpick in the center of the wheel so that you can easily turn the viewer. Line up the viewing windows so that each window is filled.

The half of the viewer, marked "Write the Equation," shows you the problem you must write as an equation. The other half of the viewer, marked "Find the Solution," shows you what step is necessary to arrive at the solution.

Turn your viewer so that an x appears in the top window of the "Write the Equation" half of the viewer.

1. Write an algebraic equation for the problem that appears in the windows.

_____

2. Did you write a multiplication or division equation? _____

3. Explain how the "Find the Solution" half of the viewer could be used to help you solve the equation. Then solve the equation.

_____

_____

Lab Activity
Equation Wheel, Chapter 6, page 2

4. Complete the chart for each of the six problems. Use the "Find the Solution" half of the viewer to help you determine the property needed to solve each equation.

Equation	Type	Property	Solution

5. Examine these equations.

a. $\frac{x}{5} = \frac{2}{15}$

b. $3x = -23$

c. $-\frac{1}{4}x = -2$

d. $-1 = \frac{x}{\frac{1}{2}}$

e. $\frac{1.2}{4} = \frac{6}{x}$

f. $-\frac{1}{5}x = 1$

Separate the viewer from the equation wheel. Turn over the equation wheel so that the blank side is facing you. Place the viewer directly over the back of the equation wheel and insert the toothpick again. Write the problem represented by each equation shown by filling in each window on the "Write the Equation" side of the viewer. Then fill in each window on the "Find the Solution" half, directly opposite the windows you just filled in. Solve each equation.

6. Make up your own equation wheel, and have a partner use his or her viewer to solve your equations.

_____

_____

_____

_____

Lab Activity
Equation Wheel, Chapter 6, page 3

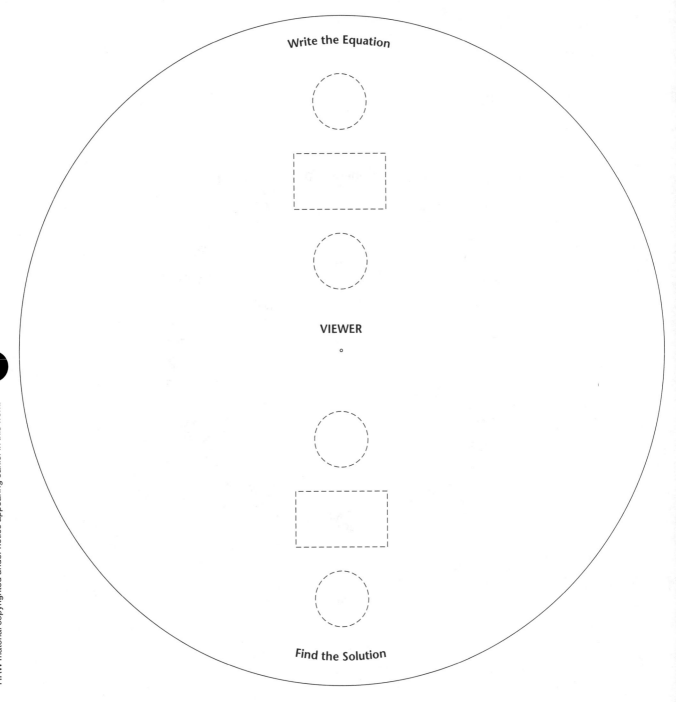

Lab Activity
Equation Wheel, Chapter 6, page 4

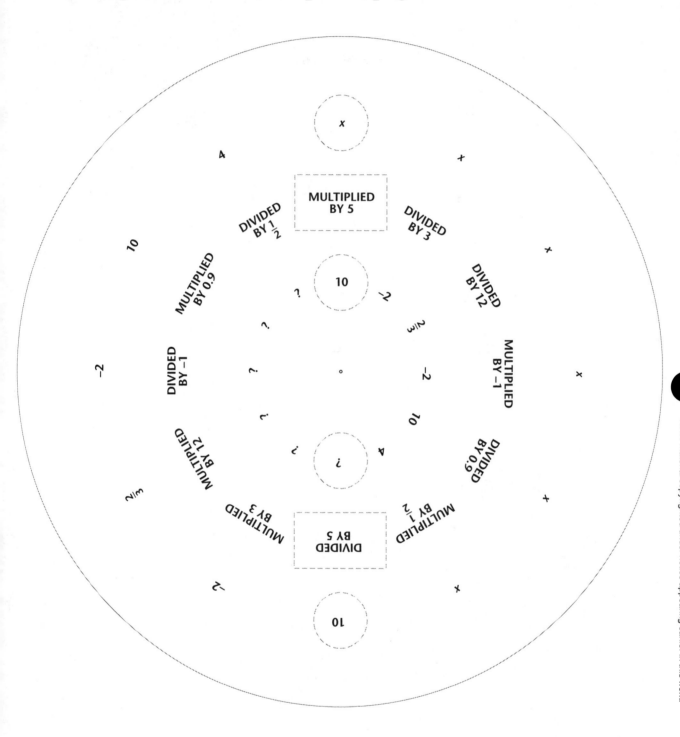

Long-Term Project
A History of Solving Proportions, Chapter 6

In every commercial transaction, a seller tries to maximize profits, and a buyer tries to get the greatest value from the purchase. Long before the cash register or computer scanner at the supermarket, people have tried to get the most for their money. Over time, mathematical methods were developed to help solve real-world problems such as measuring land, weighing and measuring produce, and paying taxes.

Most people in ancient times were unable to read or write. Before paper or writing utensils became widely available, people learned and memorized mathematical rules for solving problems. These rules were passed on by word of mouth, with no attempt to explain the underlying principles.

In this project, you will use some of these rules and see how they are the basis for solving problems by using proportions.

One of the earliest recorded formulas was the Rule of Three developed by Brahmagupta, a Hindu mathematician of the seventh century. The Rule of Three describes how to solve a problem by setting up and solving a proportion. Brahmagupta used the terms *Argument*, *Fruit*, *Requisition*, and *Produce* to write his rule:

> Requisition multiplied by Fruit and divided by Argument is Produce.

1. Write a proportion that represents Brahmagupta's Rule of Three.

_____

2. What expressions that correspond to Brahmagupta's Argument, Fruit, Requisition, and Produce might be used today?

_____

_____

Long-Term Project
A History of Solving Proportions, Chapter 6, page 2

In about 1150, another mathematician, named Bhaskara, used the Rule of Three to solve this problem:

> If two and half palas of saffron are purchased for three-sevenths of a niska, how many palas can be purchased for nine niskas?

3. Suppose $\frac{3}{7}$ and 9 represent Fruit and Produce, respectively, and $\frac{5}{2}$ represents Argument. Describe how you think Bhaskara used the Rule of Three to solve this problem.

_____

_____

4. Set up a proportion that could be used to solve this problem. Then solve your proportion.

_____

Leonardo Fibonacci was the first person to publish the Rule of Three in his book, *Liber abaci* (1202). His written presentation of this formula contributed to its spread to the rest of the world.

Fibonacci used the following problem to illustrate the Rule of Three:

> If 100 rotuli are worth 40 libras, how many libras are 5 rotuli worth?

5. Decide what values represent Argument, Fruit, and Requisition. Then use the Rule of Three to find Produce.

_____

Fibonacci extended the Rule of Three to solve this problem:

> If 5 horses eat 6 quarts of barley in 9 days, for how many days will 16 quarts feed 10 horses?

Long-Term Project
A History of Solving Proportions, Chapter 6, page 3

Fibonacci used a chart to organize the information.

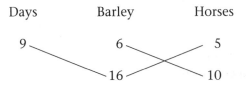

6. Write the equation that you think Fibonacci used to set up the problem.

   _____

7. Use the equation you wrote to solve the problem.

   _____

8. Set up and solve the following problem found in *Liber abaci:*

   A certain king sent 30 men into his orchard to plant trees. If they could plant 1000 trees in 9 days, in how many days would 36 men plant 4400 trees?

   _____

   _____

Around 1480 in Treviso, Italy, an anonymously published booklet contained the very earliest arithmetic ever printed. Until that time, books had been handwritten. One problem from this booklet is as follows:

   A courier travels from Rome to Venice in 7 days; another courier starts at the same time and travels from Venice to Rome in 9 days. The distance between Rome and Venice is 250 miles. In how many days will the couriers meet, and how many miles will each travel before meeting?

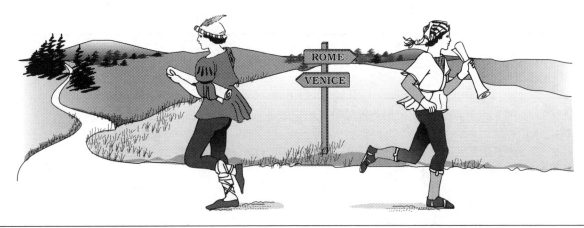

Long-Term Project
A History of Solving Proportions, Chapter 6, page 4

The Treviso booklet describes how to find the number of days it takes for the couriers to meet by adding 7 and 9 to obtain 16; then dividing 63, the product of 7 and 9, by 16, giving a result of $3\frac{15}{16}$ days.

9. Write an equation that can be used to find the number of days that it takes for the couriers to meet. Then express your equation as a proportion.

_____

To find the distance covered by the first courier, the Treviso arithmetic booklet shows the information organized in a chart.

The product of 1250, and 63 (15,750), is divided by the product of 7, 1, and 16 (112), obtaining the result $140\frac{5}{8}$ miles.

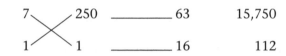

| 7 | 250 | _____ 63 | 15,750 |
| 1 | 1 | _____ 16 | 112 |

10. Use the same method to find the distance covered by the second courier.

_____

11. Describe how you can check your result.

_____

Two cars start toward each other at the same time from towns that are 270 km apart. One car averages 70 km/h, and the other averages 65 km/h. After how many hours will they pass each other? How far does each car travel before meeting?

12. How does this problem compare with the courier problem in the Treviso arithmetic booklet?

_____

13. Solve the problem.

_____

Lab Activity
Solution Slide, Chapter 7

Materials
templates for the Solution Slide
paper
scissors
tape

In this activity, you will construct a Solution Slide to solve multistep equations. The steps you use to break down equations into simpler forms can be applied to more complicated problems or data. Follow the steps below to assemble your Solution Slide.

Step 1 Cut out the templates on page 2 marked Front and Back. These templates will be used to form the Solution Slide pocket.

Step 2 To make the viewing slots for your Solution Slide pocket, cut out the areas on the Front template indicated by dotted lines.

Step 3 Tape the Front and Back templates together to complete the Solution Slide pocket.

Step 4 Cut out the blank Equation Slide template and make at least one additional copy so that you can solve equations.

Cut out the Equation Slide for the equation $5x - 8 = 3x + 12$, and insert it into the Solution Slide pocket so that the equation is at the top. The larger viewing slots show you both sides of the equation clearly divided. The smaller viewing slots are empty. As you slowly pull the Equation Slide out, the smaller viewing slots show you the strategies used to solve the equation. The larger viewing slots show you how each side of the equation is affected. Now, slowly pull the Equation Slide out.

1. Explain the steps used to solve $5x - 8 = 3x + 12$. Then tell what property each step demonstrates.

   a. _____

   b. _____

   c. _____

2. Continue to pull the Equation Slide out. Describe how to check the solution to the equation by using your Solution Slide.

   _____

Lab Activity
Solution Slide, Chapter 7, page 2

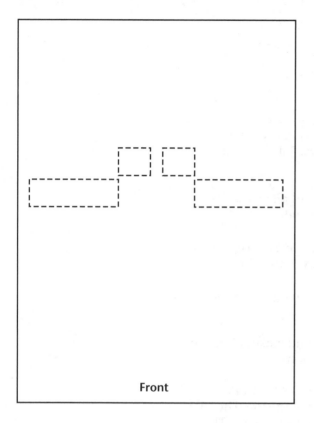

Front

Back

$5x - 8 = 3x + 12$			
$5x - 8$	$-3x$	$-3x$	$3x + 12$
$-3x + 5x - 8$			$-3x + 3x + 12$
$2x - 8$	$+ 8$	$+ 8$	12
$2x - 8 + 8$			$12 + 8$
$2x$	$\div 2$	$\div 2$	20
x	$x = 10$	$x = 10$	10
$5(10) - 8$			$3(10) + 12$
42			42

 **Lab Activity**
Solution Slide, Chapter 7, page 3

Complete each Equation Slide by showing in the smaller viewing slots what strategies you would use to solve each equation.

3.

$1 - a = 3$			
$1 - a$			3
$1 - a - 1$			$3 - 1$
$-a$			2
a			-2

4.

$\frac{t}{4} - 2 = 5$			
$\frac{t}{4} - 2$			5
$\frac{t}{4} - 2 + 2$			$5 + 2$
$\frac{t}{4}$			7
t			28

Describe the steps used to solve each equation.

5.

$4(2b - 5) = 5(b + 2)$			
$4(2b - 5)$	Distri-bute	Distri-bute	$5(b + 2)$
$8b - 20$	$-5b$	$-5b$	$5b + 10$
$8b - 5b - 20$			$5b - 5b + 10$
$3b - 20$	$+20$	$+20$	10
$3b - 20 + 20$			$10 + 20$
$3b$	$\div 3$	$\div 3$	30
b			10

6.

$4t - 1 = 2t + 3$			
$4t - 1$	$-2t$	$-2t$	$2t + 3$
$4t - 2t - 1$			$-2t + 2t + 3$
$2t - 1$	$+1$	$+1$	3
$2t - 1 + 1$			$3 + 1$
$2t$	$\div 2$	$\div 2$	4
t	$t = 2$	$t = 2$	2
$4(2) - 1$			$2(2) + 3$
7			7

a. _____

b. _____

c. _____

d. _____

a. _____

b. _____

c. _____

d. _____

Lab Activity
Solution Slide, Chapter 7, page 4

Enter the appropriate expression in each numbered slot on the Equation Slide so that the equation $3b + 9 = -2b + 29$ is solved and checked.

$3(4) + 9$	
$-2b + 29$	
29	
4	
21	
$5b$	
$29 - 9$	
$2b + 3b + 9$	
20	
$-2(4) + 29$	
$+2b$	
-9	
$5b + 9$	

$+2b$	
b	
$2b - 2b + 29$	
$3b + 9$	
21	
$5b + 9 - 9$	
$\div 5$	
$b = 4$	
-9	
$\div 5$	
$b = 4$	

Equation Slide:

$$3b + 9 = -2b + 29$$

7	15	19	23
8			24
9	16	20	25
10			26
11	17	21	27
12	18	22	28
13			29
14			30

Solve and check each equation by using your Solution Slide.

31. $2y + 1 = 5$

32. $2b - 7 = -2 + b$

_____

_____

Long-Term Project
Solving Equations in the Past, Chapter 7

Multiplication and division were invented as shortcuts for repeated addition and subtraction. Algebra was developed to handle more complicated problems in which arithmetic shortcuts were not enough. Many real-world algebra problems are similar to those problems facing people in ancient times. In this project, you will compare the ancient ways of solving problems to modern methods. Then you will draw your own conclusions about which method is easier.

The *Bakhshuli Manuscript*, written by an unknown author, was discovered in northwest India in 1881. The date of the manuscript is estimated to range from the third to the twelfth century. The following problem is found in the manuscript:

> A merchant pays a duty on certain goods at three different places. At the first place he gives $\frac{1}{3}$ of the goods, at the second place $\frac{1}{4}$ of the remainder, and at the third place $\frac{1}{5}$ of the remainder. The total duty is 24. What was the original amount of his goods?

This is the solution as it appears in the manuscript:

> Having subtracted the series from one, we get $\frac{2}{3}$, $\frac{3}{4}$, and $\frac{4}{5}$; these multiplied together give $\frac{2}{5}$; that subtracted from 1 gives $\frac{3}{5}$; with this, the total duty, 24, is divided, giving 40; that is the original amount.

Suppose you wanted to solve the same problem algebraically.

1. If x represents the original amount of goods, what expression represents the duty at the first place?

   _____

2. What expression represents the remaining goods?

   _____

3. How can you represent the duty at the second place?

   _____

One equation that models this problem is

$$\frac{1}{3}x + \frac{1}{4}\left(1 - \frac{1}{3}\right)x + \frac{1}{5}\left(1 - \frac{1}{4}\right)\left(1 - \frac{1}{3}\right)x = 24.$$

Long-Term Project
Solving Equations in the Past, Chapter 7, page 2

Explain the steps used to solve this equation.

4. $\frac{1}{3}x + \frac{1}{4}\left(1 - \frac{1}{3}\right)x + \frac{1}{5}\left(1 - \frac{1}{4}\right)\left(1 - \frac{1}{3}\right)x = 24$ _____

5. $\qquad \frac{1}{3}x + \frac{1}{4}\left(\frac{2}{3}\right)x + \frac{1}{5}\left(\frac{3}{4}\right)\left(\frac{2}{3}\right) = 24$ _____

6. $\qquad\qquad \frac{1}{3}x + \frac{1}{6}x + \frac{1}{10}x = 24$ _____

7. $\qquad\qquad\qquad \frac{3}{5}x = 24$ _____

8. $\qquad\qquad\qquad 3x = 120$ _____

9. $\qquad\qquad\qquad x = 40$ _____

The manuscript checks the solution as follows:

   $\frac{2}{5}$ multiplied by 40 gives 16 as the remainder.

   Hence the original amount is 40.

10. Describe how you would check the solution. Then check the solution.

   _____

   _____

   _____

The Hindu mathematician Mahavira (850 A.D.) wrote an elementary
mathematics book containing this problem:

   Of a collection of mango fruits, the king took $\frac{1}{6}$, the queen took

   $\frac{1}{5}$ of the remainder, the three chief princes took $\frac{1}{4}, \frac{1}{3}$, and $\frac{1}{2}$ of the

   successive remainders, and the youngest child took the remaining
   three mangoes. Oh, you who are clever in miscellaneous problems
   on fractions, give out the measure of that collection of mangoes.

11. Write an equation for finding the total number of mangoes.

   _____

12. Solve your equation. _____

13. Check your solution.

   _____

Long-Term Project
Solving Equations in the Past, Chapter 7, page 3

In his book *Liber abaci*, Fibonacci wrote this problem for readers to solve:

> A man entered an orchard through gates and there took a certain number of apples. When he left the orchard, he gave the first guard half of the apples that he had and one apple more. To the second guard, he gave half his remaining apples and one apple more. He did the same to each of the remaining five guards and left the orchard with one apple. How many apples did he gather in the orchard?

One equation you can use to solve this problem is:

$$1 + \frac{1}{2}x + 1 + \frac{1}{4}x + \frac{1}{2} + \frac{1}{8}x + \frac{1}{4} + \frac{1}{16}x + \frac{1}{8} + \frac{1}{32}x + \frac{1}{16} + \frac{1}{64}x +$$

$$\frac{1}{32} + \frac{1}{128}x + \frac{1}{64} = x$$

Complete the steps needed to solve this equation.

14. _____ Given

15. _____ Simplify.

16. _____ Subtraction Property

17. _____ Multiplication Property

Long-Term Project
Solving Equations in the Past, Chapter 7, page 4

In 1560, Bishop Carmuel, in his *Mathesis Biceps*, proposed this problem:

Half of my cattle is in such a place, $\frac{1}{8}$ in such, $\frac{1}{10}$ in such, $\frac{1}{20}$ in such $\frac{1}{60}$ in such, and here there are 50. Find the number of the herd.

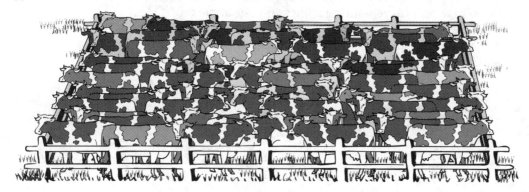

18. Write an equation to find the total number of cattle.

_____

19. Solve your equation.

_____

20. Check your solution.

_____

Use what you've learned to solve this modern-day problem.

21. Last month, Jackie spent 50% of her monthly leisure time on entertainment, 20% on exercise, 20% on crafts, and 10% on reading. Last month she spent 9 hours reading. How many hours of leisure time did Jackie have last month?

_____

_____

_____

 **Lab Activity**
Exploring Slope With Geoboards, Chapter 8

Materials
9 × 9 geoboard
rubber bands

You can use a geoboard to model the concepts you have learned in Chapter 8. The dot paper models a coordinate grid on a geoboard.

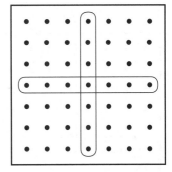

1. How are the axes represented?

   _____

2. Where is the origin located? _____

3. Look at the diagram. A rubber band is stretched between the pegs representing the point $(-2, -2)$ and $(3, 3)$. Use the formula

   $$slope = \frac{rise}{run}$$

   to find the slope of the line. _____

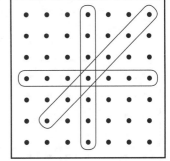

4. Choose two different pairs of points on the same line and model them on your geoboard. What is the slope of the line they represent?

   _____

5. Compare your geoboard model with the model shown. Write a generalization about the two slopes.

   _____

Model each pair of points on your geoboard. Find the slope of the line determined by each pair of points. Then show your model on the dot paper provided.

6. $(1, 2), (2, 3)$ _____   7. $(2, 0), (4, 2)$ _____

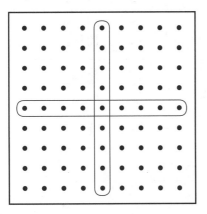   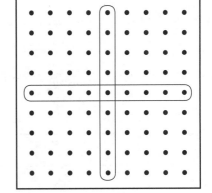

Lab Activity
Exploring Slope With Geoboards, Chapter 8, page 2

8. $(-2, -3), (3, 2)$ _____

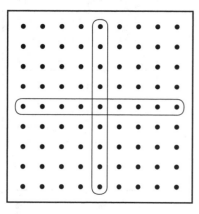

9. $(-1, -3), (-3, -4)$ _____

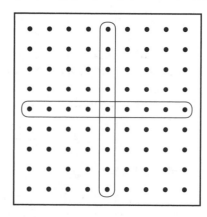

10. $(-1, -3), (-3, -1)$ _____

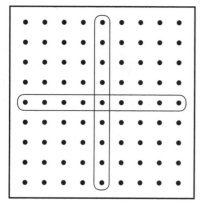

11. $(2, 0), (3, 4)$ _____

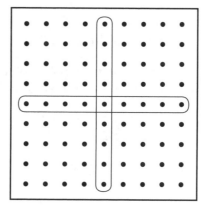

Stretch a rubber band between the points (2, 3) and (2, −3) on your geoboard. Draw your model on the dot paper provided.

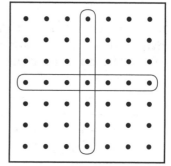

12. What is the rise? _____

13. What is the run? _____

14. What is the slope of the line? _____

15. Use the formula $slope = \dfrac{change\ in\ y}{change\ in\ x}$ to explain your answer to Exercise 14.

_____

_____

Lab Activity
Exploring Slope With Geoboards, Chapter 8, page 3

Stretch a rubber band between the points (−3, 4) and (2, 4) on your geoboard. Draw your model on the dot paper provided.

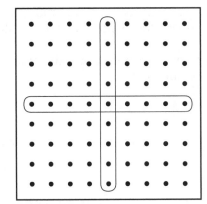

16. What is the rise? _____

17. What is the run? _____

18. What is the slope of the line? _____

19. Use the formula $slope = \frac{change\ in\ y}{change\ in\ x}$ to explain your answer for Exercise 18.

_____

_____

20. Use your geoboard to show an example of a line with no slope. Draw your model on the dot paper provided. Name the pair of points shown on your model.

_____

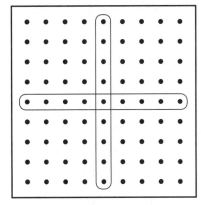

21. Use your geoboard to show an example of a line with a slope of 0. Draw your model on the dot paper provided. Name the pair of points shown on your model. What is the rise?

_____

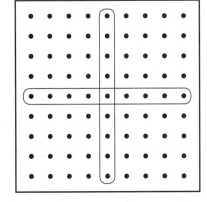

Lab Activity
Exploring Slope With Geoboards, Chapter 8, page 4

22. Use your geoboard and rubber bands to represent two parallel lines. Draw your model on the dot paper provided.

23. Find the slope of each line represented by your model, and compare them.

    Line 1 _____ Line 2 _____

    _____

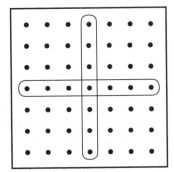

24. Show another example of parallel lines on your geoboard. Draw your model on the dot paper provided.

25. Find the slope of each line. _____

26. Write a generalization about the relationship between the slopes of any two parallel lines.

    _____

27. Use your geoboard and rubber bands to represent two perpendicular lines. Draw your model on the dot paper provided.

28. Find the slope of each line. _____

29. What is the product of the slopes? _____

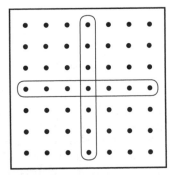

30. Show another example of perpendicular lines on your geoboard. Draw your model on the dot paper provided.

31. Find the slope of each line. _____

32. What is the product of the slopes? _____

33. Write a generalization about the relationship between the slopes of any two perpendicular lines.

    _____

HRW material copyrighted under notice appearing earlier in this work.

Long-Term Project
Hunt for the Royal Treasures, Chapter 8

Despite their fictional appearance in children's literature and fairy tales, there are countries in the world today that still have kings, queens, and other people of royal blood. In fact, there are more than four dozen reigning monarchs in countries such as Spain, Morocco, Lesotho, Nepal, and the Netherlands.

In Britain, kings and queens are descendants of royal parents. A reigning king makes his wife a queen. A reigning queen makes her husband a prince. Most royal families live in palaces.

Imagine that you have been invited to participate in a treasure hunt at the royal palace. The king informs his guests that the family's treasures were buried on the palace grounds hundreds of years ago and that only clues were left behind to locate them. Can you help the king find the royal treasures?

There are three treasures buried on the palace grounds. Use the clues to help you find them. Use the coordinate grid provided on the next page to show where they are buried.

Clues

1. The gold necklace is in a location where all the coordinates are positive.

2. The change in the y-coordinates is 7.

3. One of the y-coordinates is an even number, and its x-coordinate is an odd number.

4. None of the coordinates has two digits.

5. You can't seem to define the slope of the necklace.

6. The y-coordinate of one end of the necklace is three more than the x-coordinate.

Clues

1. A treasure chest is located in the third quadrant.

2. The lower left-hand corner of the chest lies along the line with the equation $y = x$.

3. The chest is rectangular and all four corners have odd coordinates.

4. If you looked any lower or any farther left, you'd be in the prohibited double digits.

5. The coordinates of the lower left-hand corner are the smallest you can have.

6. The chest is 6 units wide and 2 units high.

Long-Term Project
Hunt for the Royal Treasures, Chapter 8, page 2

Clues

1. The crown is buried at an angle.

2. All the *x*-coordinates are positive, and all the *y*-coordinates are negative.

3. The top of the crown is parallel to the bottom of the crown, and the the top and bottom are the same length.

4. The top and bottom each have one point with odd coordinates and another point with even coordinates.

5. The difference of the *y*-coordinates is 3, and the difference of the *x*-coordinates is 3.

6. The corners of the top are located 1 unit north and 1 unit west of the bottom corners.

7. One of the top corners is located where the lines $y = -3$ and $x = 7$ meet.

8. None of the corners has a coordinate of 0.

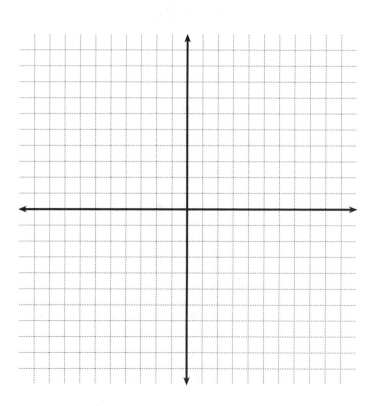

Long-Term Project
Hunt for the Royal Treasures, Chapter 8, page 3

1. Where is the gold necklace buried? Draw it on the coordinate grid on the previous page. Then list its coordinates.

   _____

2. Where is the treasure chest buried? Draw it on the coordinate grid on the previous page. Then list its coordinates.

   _____

3. Where is the crown buried? Draw it on the coordinate grid on the previous page. Then list its coordinates.

   _____

Now create your own treasure hunt game by using the concepts you learned in Chapter 8. Begin by deciding the rules of the game. Will the opponents take turns guessing the location of the objects? Will the players work independently? How will you use slopes to determine the location of the hidden treasures?

Once you have outlined your plan you may go back and rework any aspect of the game. Then play your game with an opponent to see if it is challenging enough!

TITLE OF GAME: _____

NUMBER OF PLAYERS: _____

OBJECT OF GAME: _____

_____

HOW TO PLAY:

_____

_____

_____

_____

_____

_____

Long-Term Project
Hunt for the Royal Treasures, Chapter 8, page 4

Clues	Clues

Make additional clue cards as needed.

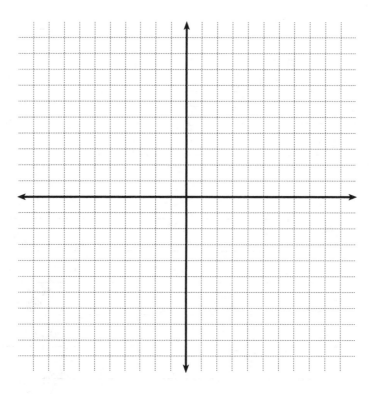

Lab Activity
Solving Systems With Algebra Tiles, Chapter 9

Materials
positive and negative *x*-tiles and *y*-tiles
positive and negative unit tiles

In this activity, you will use algebra tiles to solve systems of equations by substitution and by elimination by multiplication.

1. Use tiles to represent this system of equations.

$$\begin{cases} x + 2y = 4 \\ 2x + 3y = 6 \end{cases}$$

Sketch your representation in the diagram.

2. Describe how you would solve the first equation for *x*. What is your result?

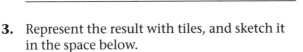

_____

_____

3. Represent the result with tiles, and sketch it in the space below.

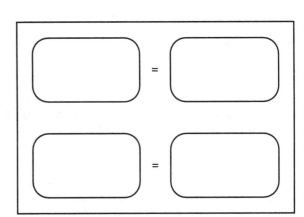

4. Use the tiles that represent *x* in the equation from Exercise 3 and substitute them for *x* in the second equation. Since the second equation calls for 2*x*, you will need to double the tiles that represent *x*. Sketch your result in the diagram.

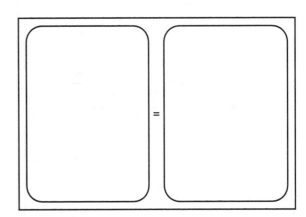

5. Describe how you would solve this equation for *y*. What is the result?

_____

_____

Lab Activity
Solving Systems With Algebra Tiles, Chapter 9, page 2

6. Use your result to substitute the correct number of unit tiles for y in the original version of the first equation. Since the equation calls for $2y$, you will need to double the tiles that represent y. Sketch your result.

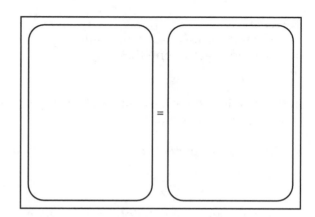

7. Describe how you would solve the equation for x. What is the result?

_____

_____

8. How could you check your answer?

_____

Use the same process to solve the system of equations below. Use the diagrams to sketch the tiles that you use in each step.

9. $\begin{cases} x - 3y = 3 \\ 2x - 4y = 8 \end{cases}$ _____

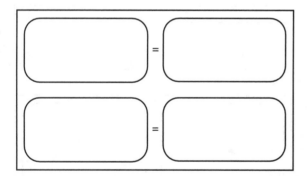
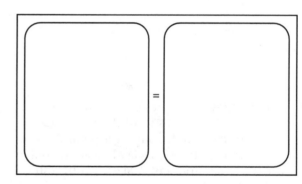
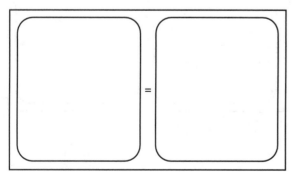
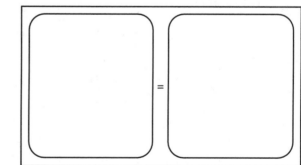

Lab Activity
Solving Systems With Algebra Tiles, Chapter 9, page 3

In Lesson 9.3 you learned how to use algebra tiles to solve systems of equations by using elimination by addition. Use the same concepts to solve the problems by elimination by multiplication.

10. Use algebra tiles to represent this system of equations.

$$\begin{cases} 2x + 3y = 7 \\ -3x + 3y = -3 \end{cases}$$

Sketch your representation in the diagram.

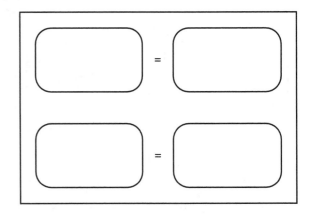

11. By what number should you multiply the second equation in order to eliminate the $3y$ terms by addition?

_____

12. Multiply the second equation by the number you found in Exercise 11. Represent the equation with algebra tiles. In the top two sections of the diagram, sketch representations of the first equation in its original form and the second equation in the form you just created.

13. Add the two equations, and represent the resulting equation with algebra tiles. Complete the diagram with a sketch of this equation.

14. Solve the resulting equation. What is the result?

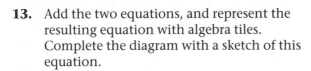

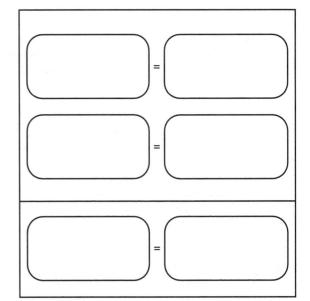

15. Use your result to substitute the correct number of unit tiles for x in one of the original equations, and solve for y.

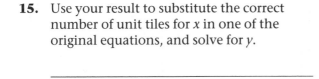

_____

_____

Lab Activity
Solving Systems With Algebra Tiles, Chapter 9, page 4

16. Use the same process to solve the following system of equations:

$$\begin{cases} 5y - 2x = 3 \\ 2y + 4x = -18 \end{cases}$$ _____

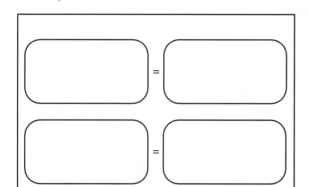

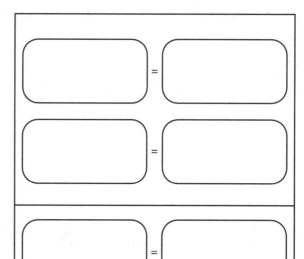

17. Create a system of equations that can be solved by elimination by multiplication. Write the system of equations in the space provided. Sketch the steps needed to solve your system with algebra tiles. Include the solution.

System of equations: _____   Solution: _____

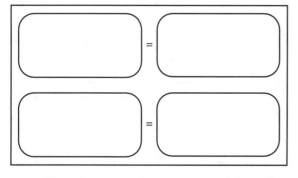

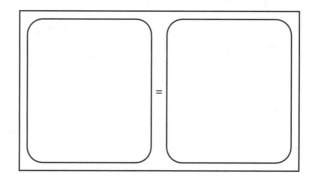

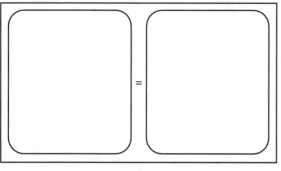

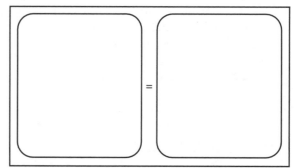

Long-Term Project
Using Systems in Business, Chapter 9

Chris owns an automobile dealership. As he makes decisions about his investments, inventory, and other business practices, he often uses systems of equations. Use your knowledge of solving systems of equations to help Chris with his business decisions.

First briefly describe how to use each method below for solving a system of equations.

1. graphing

_____

2. substitution

_____

3. elimination by addition or subtraction

_____

4. elimination by multiplication

_____

For each problem in which you solve a system of equations, choose one of the processes above and explain the reasons for your choice.

5. Every Monday, Chris takes inventory of the lot. Chris's inventory includes both cars and trucks. The average price of a car on the lot is $17,500, and the average price of a truck on the lot is $22,300. If Chris's total inventory of cars and trucks is equal to $1,855,600 at this time, write an equation, using c as the number of cars and t as the number of trucks, that represents his inventory.

_____

6. Chris counts the total number of vehicles on the lot and finds that he has exactly 100 vehicles. Write an equation, using c as the number of cars and t as the number of trucks, that represents his inventory.

_____

Long-Term Project
Using Systems in Business, Chapter 9, page 2

7. Use your equations to calculate the number of cars and the number of trucks that Chris currently has on the lot.

_____

8. Which process did you use to solve your system of equations? Why?

_____

Chris has decided to add minivans to his inventory because they are very popular with families. On Tuesday, he received a large shipment of minivans. Chris is going to consider minivans as part of the car inventory. This means that the car section of the lot would include both minivans and other cars.

9. After adding the new shipment of minivans to the cars, Chris finds that he has 100 vehicles in the car section of the lot. Write an equation, using m as the number of minivans and c as the number of other cars, that represents his current car inventory.

_____

10. The accountant informs Chris that the car inventory is now worth $1,972,500. If the average price of a minivan is $26,400, write an equation, using m as the number of minivans and c as the number of other cars, that represents the value of the car inventory.

_____

11. Use your equations to calculate the number of minivans and the number of other cars that Chris currently has on the lot.

_____

12. Which process did you use to solve this system of equations? Why?

_____

13. According to your new count, how many cars did Chris sell between Monday and Tuesday?

_____

Long-Term Project
Using Systems in Business, Chapter 9, page 3

14. If no trucks have been sold between Monday and Tuesday, what is the value of Chris's complete inventory on Tuesday?

_____

15. On Wednesday, Chris receives a shipment of 3 new trucks. What is the new value of his truck inventory? (Use the average price for trucks.)

_____

16. Chris has noticed that customers seem to like the one-price concept, in which the dealer offers one price to every customer regardless of his or her bargaining ability. He would like to try this idea in the truck section. He has two different models of trucks. The smaller one is priced at $21,400, and the larger one is priced at $23,650. Write an equation, using s for the small trucks and b for the big trucks, that represents the total dollar value of the truck section, based on your calculations for Exercise 15.

_____

17. Write an equation representing the number of small trucks and the number of big trucks in the truck section at Chris's dealership.

_____

18. Use your equations to calculate the number of small trucks and the number of big trucks that Chris has on the lot.

_____

19. Which process did you use to solve this system of equations? Why?

_____

_____

20. Chris's business has been booming since he instituted the one-price concept in the truck section. He would like to do the same thing in the car section with the cars that are not minivans. The cars are a mix of economy and sports cars. The price for the economy cars will be $16,400, and the price for the sports cars will be $21,900. Write two equations that can be used to find the number of economy cars, e, and the number of sports cars, s.

_____

Long-Term Project
Using Systems in Business, Chapter 9, page 4

21. Solve your system of equations to find the number of economy cars and the number of sports cars.

_____

22. Which process did you use to solve this system of equations? Why?

_____

23. Design your own car dealership by using systems of equations to help you decide on your inventory. You may use fictional prices and models of vehicles, or you may research actual prices of models sold in your area. Start by deciding on a total dollar value for the inventory that you wish to keep on your lot. Then decide on the total number of vehicles that you wish to keep on your lot. Next you need to determine average prices for the sections or models of vehicles on your lot. Work with two sections or models at a time so that you will generate and solve systems of two equations. Describe your lot's situation and how you used systems of equations to make decisions. Also tell which processes you used to solve your systems of equations and why you chose those processes.

Total dollar value _____

Total number of vehicles _____

Other descriptions or information _____

_____

_____

_____

24. How did you use systems of equations to set up your car lot?

_____

_____

25. Which processes did you use to solve your systems of equations? Why did you choose these processes over the other options?

_____

_____

Lab Activity
Finding the Area of Polygons, Chapter 10

Materials
square dot paper, or geoboard and rubber bands
isometric dot paper
hexagonal dot paper

The area of the smallest square on square dot paper is 1 square unit. To find the area of the polygon shown you can divide the area into smaller triangular regions, find the area of each region, and find the sum of the areas to find the area of the polygon.

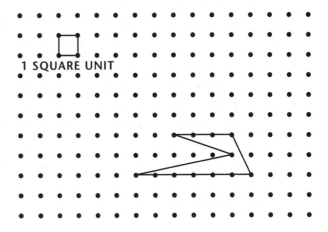

For example, region I is a triangle whose base is 3 units and height is 1 unit. So, the area of region I is $\frac{1}{2}$(base)(height) = $\frac{1}{2}$(3)(1) = 1.5 square units.

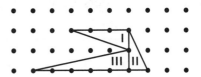

1. Find the area of region II and region III. Then use the areas of the three regions to find the area of the polygon in the example.

_____

_____

For some polygons, using the standard formulas for area would be difficult. Calculating area by counting the number of dots on the edge of the polygon would be much easier.

In this activity, you will discover a function that relates the area of a polygon to the number of dots on its boundary when there are no dots inside the polygon.

Lab Activity
Finding the Area of Polygons, Chapter 10, page 2

Find the area of each polygon and complete the table. Look for a pattern in your answers.

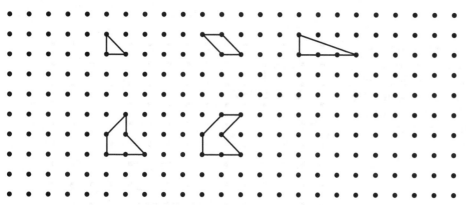

2.

Boundary dots	3	4	5	6	7
Area					

3. Predict the area of a polygon if it has exactly 11 dots on its boundary and no interior dots. Draw a polygon to check your prediction.

_____

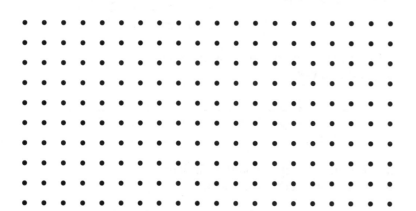

4. Write a rule for finding the area as a function of the number of boundary dots, *n*, on square dot paper when the number of interior dots is 0. Then check your rule by finding the area of the polygon in the example on the previous page.

_____

_____

_____

Lab Activity
Finding the Area of Polygons, Chapter 10, page 3

Find the area of each polygon with one interior dot. Complete the table
and look for the pattern in your answers.

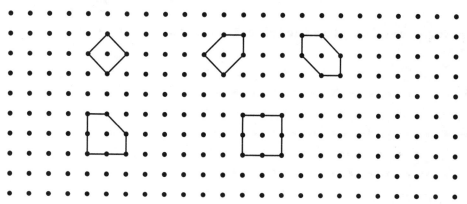

5.

Boundary dots	3	4	5	6	7
Area					

6. Predict the area of a polygon that has exactly 12 dots on its boundary
and one interior dot. Draw a polygon to check your prediction.

_____

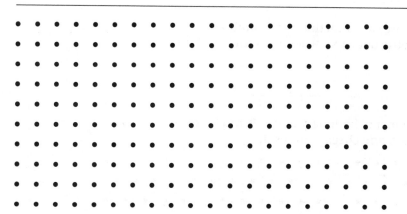

7. Write a rule for finding the area as a function of the number of
boundary dots, *n,* on square dot paper when the number of interior
dots is exactly one.

_____

_____

8. How does this rule compare with the rule you wrote for Exercise 4?

_____

_____

Lab Activity
Finding the Area of Polygons, Chapter 10, page 4

These dots are on isometric dot paper. The area of one equilateral triangle is 1 square unit.

Find the area of each polygon and complete the table. Look for a pattern in your answers.

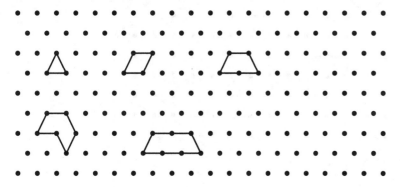

9.

Boundary dots	3	4	5	6	7
Area					

10. Write a rule for finding the area as a function of the number of boundary dots, n, on isometric dot paper when the number of interior dots is 0.

_____

11. Find the area when the number of boundary dots is 9 and there are no interior dots. Draw a polygon and check your result.

Long-Term Project
Vacation Time, Chapter 10

Keesha is planning a vacation for the summer after she graduates from high school. Her family has agreed to pay for her air fare and hotel accommodations if she saves enough money for the rental car and pocket money. Keesha decides that she will use the money she has saved from her part-time job as spending money, and she will use the interest earned in her savings account to pay for the rental car.

Keesha needs to research how much interest she can earn and how much a car might cost to rent. She begins by researching banks and interest rates.

She decides that she wants to deposit $1000 in an account at a bank that pays compound interest. Compound interest is paid on both the principal and any previously earned interest. Banks pay interest on savings accounts at specific interest periods, which can be monthly, quarterly, semiannually, or annually. Interest rates also vary between banks.

Before she begins shopping for a new bank, Keesha decides to do her own calculations so that she can be more informed when meeting with a banker.

To find the compound interest, she uses the formula $A = P\left(1 + \frac{r}{n}\right)^{nt}$ where

A is the amount in the account, P is the principal, r is the annual interest rate, n is the number of interests periods per year, and t is time in years.

For example, Keesha wants to see how much interest she would earn in 2 years at a rate of 4% if the interest is compounded semiannually.

$$A = 1000\left(1 + \frac{0.04}{2}\right)^{2(2)} = 1000(1 + 0.02)^4$$

$$= 1000(1.02)^4$$

$$= 1000(1.0824322) \approx 1082.4322$$

Keesha would earn about $82.43 over a two-year period. She anticipates that the rental car will cost more than $82.43 and decides that her money needs to earn more interest.

Find the amount, A, for each of the following by using the compound interest formula. Assume that there are no deposits or withdrawals after the initial deposit of $1000. Then record your answers in the chart.

1. Find A if $P = \$1000$, $r = 3\%$, $n = 2$, and $t = 2$.

_____

Long-Term Project
Vacation Time, Chapter 10, page 2

2. Find A if $P = \$1000$, $r = 4\%$, $n = 4$, and $t = 2$.

_____

3. Find A if $P = \$1000$, $r = 5\%$, $n = 2$, and $t = 2$.

_____

4. Find A if $P = \$1000$, $r = 5.5\%$, $n = 12$, and $t = 2$.

_____

5. Find A if $P = \$1000$, $r = 6\%$, $n = 1$, and $t = 2$.

_____

6. Find A if $P = \$1000$, $r = 7\%$, $n = 2$, and $t = 2$.

_____

7. Find A if $P = \$1000$, $r = 8.2\%$, $n = 4$, and $t = 2$.

_____

8. Find A if $P = \$1000$, $r = 9\%$, $n = 1$, and $t = 2$.

_____

9.

Principal	Rate	Number of interest periods per year	Time	Amount in account	Interest earned

Long-Term Project
Vacation Time, Chapter 10, page 3

Call or visit at least five banking institutions in your community. Find out their policies on compound interest. Then calculate the interest earned on $1000 over 2 years at their given rates and number of interest periods per year. Complete the chart.

10.

Name of bank	Principal	Number of interest periods per year	Time	Amount in account

11. Using the information in the chart, what is the average interest rate

that most banks offer? _____

12. About how much interest do you think Keesha will earn over a 2-year

period? _____

Car-rental companies usually charge a flat rate per day or a special weekend rate. In addition, some companies offer unlimited miles, and some charge an additional per-mile rate after a certain number of free miles per day. Contact four different car-rental companies, and find out their rates for a one-week rental of a compact car. Try to get a variety of rates and billing conditions. Record your information in a table of values. Then graph the ordered pairs on the grids provided.

13. Name of car-rental company: _____

Miles	Dollars

Long-Term Project
Vacation Time, Chapter 10, page 4

14. Name of car-rental company: _____

Miles	Dollars

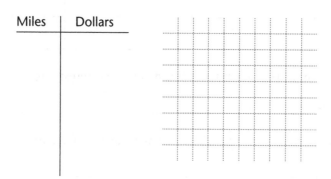

15. Name of car-rental company: _____

Miles	Dollars

16. Name of car-rental company: _____

Miles	Dollars

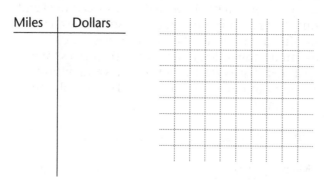

17. Which graphs represent linear functions? Why? _____

18. Which graphs represent non-constant linear functions? Why? _____

19. Review all of the data you have gathered. What recommendation would you make to Keesha about making a rental-car choice based on the price of the rental car and the amount of money she can afford to pay for it? Explain your response.

_____

Lab Activity
Tangram Statistics, Chapter 11

Materials
one set of tangrams
stopwatch or watch with a timer

In this activity you will present 15 people with a tangram puzzle and time how long it takes each person to complete the puzzle. Afterward, you will analyze the data that you collect in order to complete a statistical report. If you do not have tangrams, you can construct a set by tracing the shapes shown at right onto cardboard and cutting out the shapes.

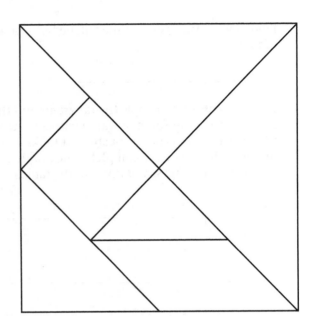

1. Create a design that uses all seven pieces. Try to make your design complicated enough so that it will take someone else a little time to reproduce it. Trace the outline (outside edge) of your design in the space provided below.

Lab Activity
Tangram Statistics, Chapter 11, page 2

2. Predict what the average time will be for people to complete your tangram puzzle.

_____

3. Give each of the 15 people the tangrams and the outline of your design. Use a stopwatch or watch with a timer to time each person from the moment that he or she first looks at the outline to the moment that he or she completes the puzzle correctly. Record the 15 people's names, ages, and times in the table.

Subject #	Name	Age	Time
1			
2			
3			
4			
5			
6			
7			
8			
9			
10			
11			
12			
13			
14			
15			

4. Calculate the mean time. _____

5. What is the median time? _____

6. What is the mode of the times? _____

 **Lab Activity**
Tangram Statistics, Chapter 11, page 3

7. What is the range of the times? _____

8. How does the calculated mean compare with your prediction? _____

_____

9. What is the mean age of the people who took part in your study? _____

10. What is the median age? _____

11. What is the mode of the ages? _____

12. What is the range of the ages? _____

13. Repeat the process with a different tangram design of the same level
of difficulty. Try to use a different set of people if possible.

14. Predict the amount of time that it will take these people to solve your new puzzle. _____

15. Record your data in the table.

Subject #	Name	Age	Time
1			
2			
3			
4			
5			
6			
7			
8			
9			
10			
11			
12			
13			
14			
15			

Lab Activity
Tangram Statistics, Chapter 11, page 4

16. Calculate the mean time. _____

17. What is the median time? _____

18. What is the mode of the times? _____

19. What is the range of the times? _____

20. How does the calculated mean compare with your prediction?

_____

21. Calculate the mean age. _____

22. What is the median age? _____

23. What is the mode of the ages? _____

24. What is the range of the ages? _____

25. Write a comparison between the two studies that you conducted. Be sure to compare times, ages, accuracy of your predictions, and other relevant information.

_____

_____

_____

26. Choose whether to display your results with a stem-and-leaf plot, histogram, box-and-whisker plot, or circle graph. Explain why you think the method you chose is appropriate.

_____

_____

27. Make a scatter plot of your data on a sheet of grid paper. Determine whether there seems to be a correlation between age and time needed to complete the puzzle.

_____

28. How could a similar study that times how long it takes students to read a paragraph be used by a teacher?

_____

Long-Term Project
Sweet Statistics, Chapter 11

Verel is a high school student taking algebra. He loves
Rainbow Fruit Snacks and buys a package almost every
day. He has noticed that sometimes it seems like there
are fewer fruit snacks in a package than other times. He
has also noticed that the number of fruit snacks of each
color is not always the same. His algebra teacher has
assigned a project in which each student must do a
statistical study of something in his or her everyday life.
Verel has decided to study the statistics of Rainbow Fruit
Snacks.

In this project, you will use your knowledge of statistics
to help Verel analyze samples of fruit snacks.

Verel bought 20 packages of fruit snacks and counted the
number of fruit snacks in each package. The table shows the
data that Verel collected.

Package #	# of fruit snacks	Package #	# of fruit snacks
1	20	11	26
2	22	12	21
3	19	13	21
4	20	14	23
5	26	15	24
6	18	16	19
7	19	17	23
8	21	18	22
9	23	19	26
10	25	20	22

1. What is the mean number of fruit snacks in a package based on the
   20 packages that Verel bought?

   _____

2. Explain the process you used to find the mean.

   _____

3. What is the median number of fruit snacks in a package based on the
   20 packages that Verel bought?

   _____

4. Explain the process you used to find the median.

   _____

Long-Term Project
Sweet Statistics, Chapter 11, page 2

5. Find the mode(s) for Verel's data. _____

6. Explain the process you used to find the mode(s).

_____

7. What is the range of the number of fruit snacks in the 20

packages? _____

8. Explain the process you used to find the range.

_____

9. Use the grid below and the data from Verel's table to create a
histogram. Use intervals of 2 for the number of fruit snacks per
package.

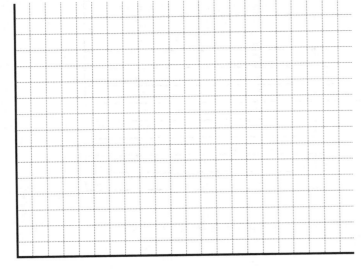

Number of fruit snacks per package

10. Find the upper and lower quartiles for the data from Verel's table.

_____

11. Use the data from Verel's table to create a box-and-whisker plot in the
space provided.

Long-Term Project
Sweet Statistics, Chapter 11, page 3

Verel also collected data about the colors of the fruit snacks in the packages. He counted the number of each color for each of the 20 packages and recorded the data in a table.

Package #	Colors					
	Purple	Green	Yellow	Blue	Red	Orange
1	3	2	4	7	3	1
2	4	2	4	7	3	2
3	3	1	4	7	3	1
4	2	3	4	6	3	2
5	4	3	5	7	5	2
6	3	2	2	7	3	1
7	3	3	3	6	2	2
8	1	5	7	4	1	3
9	2	4	1	5	7	4
10	5	5	2	5	5	3
11	4	3	3	8	4	4
12	2	4	7	4	2	2
13	3	4	6	3	3	2
14	4	4	6	4	3	2
15	4	4	5	6	2	3
16	3	1	4	7	3	1
17	2	4	1	6	6	4
18	4	2	4	6	3	3
19	4	4	4	6	6	2
20	5	1	4	5	3	4

Calculate the mean for each color. Round your result to the nearest whole number.

12. purple _____ **13.** green _____ **14.** yellow _____

15. blue _____ **16.** red _____ **17.** orange _____

18. Using the means you calculated, how many total fruit snacks would

be in a package consisting of the mean number of each color? _____

Using this number of total fruit snacks and the mean number of each color, determine the percent of the total package for each of the color. Round your results to the nearest percent.

19. purple _____ **20.** green _____ **21.** yellow _____

22. blue _____ **23.** red _____ **24.** orange _____

Long-Term Project
Sweet Statistics, Chapter 11, page 4

25. Use your calculations to construct a circle graph to represent the package containing the mean number of each color. Be sure to label the sections of your circle graph with the appropriate color.

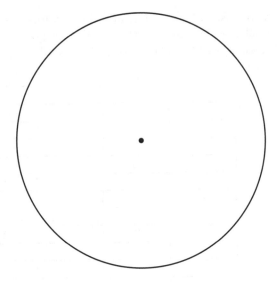

Assuming that the same percent would be represented in a larger package of fruit snacks, how many fruit snacks of each color would there be in a package of 300 fruit snacks?

26. purple _____

27. green _____

28. yellow _____

29. blue _____

30. red _____

31. orange _____

32. Based on the data in Verel's table, which color or colors have the

greatest range? _____

33. What is the mode of the yellow fruit snacks? _____

34. What is the median of the blue fruit snacks? _____

35. Choose a situation of your own for which you could conduct a similar statistical analysis. Describe your situation in the space provided. Be sure to include a description of what statistical calculations and graphs would be useful.

_____

_____

_____

_____

Lab Activity
3-D Geometry, Chapter 12

Materials
fillable cube, pyramid, cylinder, cone, and sphere
large container with pour spout
funnel
water
one-quart or one-liter measuring cup
wrapping paper, newsprint, construction paper, or plain paper
scissors
ruler

In this activity, you will use fillable, three-dimensional shapes to learn
about area and volume. The cone and cylinder should have the same radius
and height. The sphere should also have the same radius. The cube and the
pyramid should have the same height and congruent square bases.

1. Trace the circular base of the cylinder or cone on a piece of paper.

   Measure the diameter of the base. _____

2. Find the circumference of the base, and explain how you calculated it.

   _____

3. Find the area of the base, and explain how you calculated it.

   _____

4. Wrap the sides of the cylinder with paper. Trim
   the paper so that it fits exactly around the sides
   of the cylinder. Remove the paper and lay it flat
   on your desk. What familiar shape does the
   paper make?

   _____

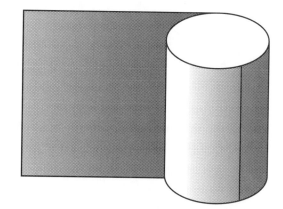

5. Find the area of this shape, and explain how
   you calculated it.

   _____

   _____

6. The top base of the cylinder is identical to the bottom base of the
   cylinder. The total surface area can be found by adding the areas of the
   top and bottom bases and the area of the shape that makes up the

   cylinder's sides. What is the surface area of the cylinder?_____

Lab Activity
3-D Geometry, Chapter 12, page 2

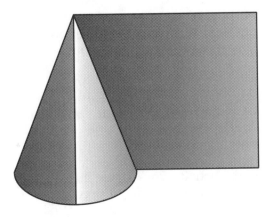

7. Wrap the sides of the cone with paper. Trim the paper so that it fits exactly around the sides of the cone. Remove the paper and lay it flat on your desk. What shape does the paper make?

_____

8. Find the area of this shape, and explain how you calculated it. Remember that this shape represents the lateral surface area of the cone.

_____

_____

9. The total surface area of the cone can be found by adding the area of the base of the cone and the area of the sides of the cone. What is the

surface area of the cone? _____

10. Fill the cylinder with water. Pour the water from the cylinder into the measuring cup. What is the volume of the water that fills

the cylinder? _____

11. Fill the cone with water. Pour the water from the cone into the measuring cup. What is the volume of the water that fills the

cone? _____

12. How do the volumes of the cylinder and cone compare?

_____

13. If the formula for the volume of a cylinder is $\pi r^2 h$, where r is the radius and h is the height of the cylinder, what would be the formula

for the volume of a cone? _____

14. Trace the base of the cube or pyramid on a piece of paper. Measure the

lengths of the sides of the traced base. _____

15. Find the perimeter of the base, and explain how you calculated it.

_____

Lab Activity
3-D Geometry, Chapter 12, page 3

16. Find the area of the base, and explain how you calculated it.

_____

17. Wrap the sides of the cube with paper. Trim the paper so that it fits exactly around the sides of the cube. Remove the paper and lay it flat on your desk. What familiar shape is each side of the cube?

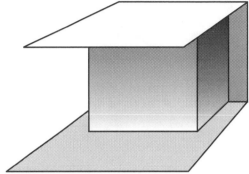

_____

18. The sides of the cube are identical. The total surface area can be found by multiplying the area of one of the sides by six. What is the surface area of the cube?

_____

19. Wrap the sides of the pyramid with paper. Trim the paper so that it fits exactly around the sides of the pyramid. Remove the paper and lay it flat on your desk. What familiar shape is each side of the pyramid?

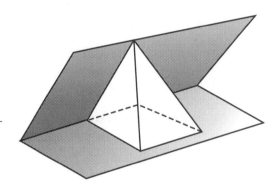

_____

20. Find the area of each side of the pyramid, and explain how you calculated it.

_____

_____

21. The total surface area of the pyramid can be found by adding the areas of the sides of the pyramid and the area of the base of the pyramid. What is the surface area of the pyramid?

_____

22. Fill the cube with water. Pour the water from the cube into the measuring cup. What is the volume of the water that fills the cube?

_____

Lab Activity
3-D Geometry, Chapter 12, page 4

23. Fill the pyramid with water. Pour the water from the pyramid into the measuring cup. What is the volume of the water that fills the

pyramid? _____

24. How do the volumes of the cube and pyramid compare?

_____

25. If the formula for the volume of the cube is s^3, where s is the length of a side of the cube, what would be the formula for the volume of the

pyramid? _____

26. The diameter of the sphere should be the same as the diameter of the base of the cone and cylinder. Write the measurements of the diameter and the radius of the sphere.

_____

27. The formula for the surface area of a sphere is $4\pi r^2$. What is the

surface area of the sphere? _____

28. Fill the cone with water. Empty the cone into the sphere. Continue to fill the cone and empty it into the sphere until the sphere is full. How many cones did it take to fill the

sphere? _____

29. The ice-cream cone shown to the right is in the shape of a cone with a hemisphere on top. If the both the cone and hemisphere are full of ice cream, what is the total volume of the ice cream?

_____

30. A monument consists of a pyramid on top of a cube. The artist would like to cover the monument until the official unveiling ceremony. The height of both the cube and the pyramid is 4 feet, and the slant height of the pyramid is 4.5 feet. What is the surface area of the monument that needs to be covered?

_____

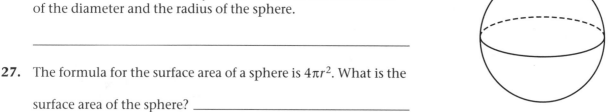

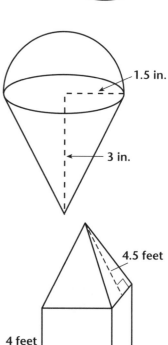

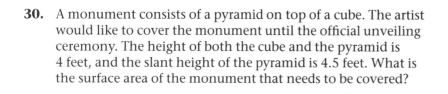

Long-Term Project
Digging Volumes, Chapter 12

Engineers often need to use area, volume, and surface area when determining the amount of dirt to remove from a site for a new structure. In many cases the volume of dirt to be removed is in the shape of a regular solid, such as a cube or cylinder. For each of the situations in this project, use your knowledge of geometric solids to answer the questions.

1. The plans for a new home require that a basement area be dug to extend under half of the house, with a crawl space under the other half of the house. The basement pit will be 18-feet long, 18-feet wide, and 9-feet deep. Sketch the basement pit in the space provided. Be sure to label all dimensions.

2. The volume of the pit can be modeled by four 9-foot cubes.

   What is the volume of one of these cubes? _____

3. What is the total volume of the basement pit? _____

Long-Term Project
Digging Volumes, Chapter 12, page 2

4. The machinery being used can move approximately 27 cubic feet with one scoop. How many scoops will it take to dig out the basement pit?

_____

5. The crawl space under the house requires a pit that is 5 feet deep. Since the basement covers half the base of the house, the crawl space is also 18-feet long by 18-feet wide. What volume of dirt must be removed

   to clear this section? _____

6. If the same digging machinery is used, about how many scoops will it

   take to remove the dirt for the crawl space? _____

7. Sketch the entire basement and crawl space in the space provided. Be sure to label all dimensions.

8. What is the total volume of the dirt that must be removed to clear the

   entire basement and crawl space? _____

9. The dump truck on the site can hold approximately 324 cubic feet. How many truck loads of dirt must be removed to clear the basement

   and crawl space? _____

10. The pits must be lined with a cement foundation. Calculate the surface area that requires lining. Keep in mind that all of the dirt walls and floors need to be lined. Assume that there is no wall separating the basement and crawl space.

_____

11. What is the area of the base of the house? _____

Long-Term Project
Digging Volumes, Chapter 12, page 3

12. If the cement lining of the basement crawl space is 6 inches thick, what are the dimensions inside the basement and the crawl space?

_____

13. What is the total volume inside the basement? _____

14. What is the total volume inside the crawl space? _____

Solve each problem. Round answers to the nearest tenth.

15. Sign posts and large poles require large supports, which are often built underground. A telephone pole, for example, may need to be supported by concrete 5 feet under the ground. If the hole for the telephone pole needs to be 3 feet in diameter and 5 feet deep, what volume of dirt must be removed?

_____

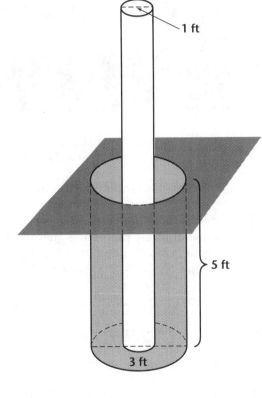

1 ft

5 ft

3 ft

16. To keep the concrete from seeping into the dirt, a plastic liner is used. Calculate the surface area of the liner that covers the floor and walls of the hole.

_____

17. If the pole has a diameter of 1 foot and rests on the ground at the bottom of the hole, what is the volume of the section of the pole that will be surrounded by concrete?

_____

18. Use your results to determine the volume of concrete needed to fill the hole around the pole.

_____

19. Once the pole is in place and the concrete has set, dirt and sod are placed over the concrete around the base of the pole. How many square feet of dirt and sod will be needed to cover this area? _____

Long-Term Project
Digging Volumes, Chapter 12, page 4

Suppose that the depth of the hole is increased to 6 feet. Calculate each of the following based on this new depth.

20. volume of dirt to be removed _____

21. surface area of plastic lining needed _____

22. volume of pole underground _____

23. volume of concrete needed to fill the hole around the pole _____

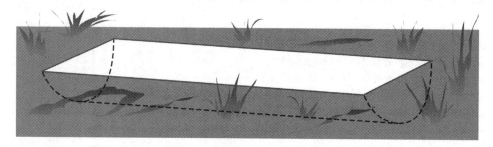

24. A drainage ditch is often modeled by half of a cylinder. This creates a solid shape with semicircular bases. Calculate the volume of half of a

cylinder with a radius of 4 feet and a length of 30 feet. _____

25. A crew is hired to dig a drainage ditch in the median of a section of divided highway that is one-quarter of a mile long. The ditch will be 20 feet in diameter and stretch the entire length of the highway section. Calculate the volume of the ditch. Remember that one mile is

5280 feet. _____

26. If the ditch is expanded to run along 15 miles of the highway, what is

the total volume of the ditch? _____

27. If this entire ditch is to be lined with sod, how many square feet of

sod would be necessary? _____

28. The ends of the ditch, where the divided highway returns to undivided highway, must be half-cone sections. The diameter of the ditch narrows from 20 feet to a point over a distance of 660 feet. What would be the volume of each half-cone section of the ditch?

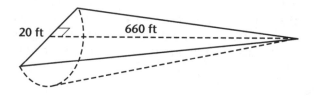

_____

ANSWERS

Lab Activity—Chapter 1

1. c **2.** e **3.** b **4.** a **5.** d

6. Possible answer: 3 and 2

7. Yes. Possible answer: 1 by 6

8. There should be two rectangles: one 2 cm by 3 cm and the other 1 cm by 6 cm.

9. 1, 2, 3, 6 **10.** 2 and 3 **11.** $2 \cdot 3$

12. 4 cm by 5 cm, or 2 cm by 10 cm

13. Student sketches should show one of the two rectangles described in Exercise 12.

14. 4 or 10

15–16. If the answer was 4, the dimensions are 2 cm by 2 cm, and there should be a sketch of a 2-cm-by-2-cm square. If the answer was 10, the dimensions are 2 cm by 5 cm, and there should be a sketch of a 2-cm-by-5-cm rectangle.

17. $2 \cdot 2 \cdot 5$ **18.** $2^2 \cdot 5$

19. Students should sketch a rectangular prism labeled 2 cm by 2 cm by 5 cm.

20. Students should use any pair of factors of 54 except 54 and 1. Possible answer: 3 cm by 18 cm. Their sketches should show a rectangle with the factors as the dimensions.

21. Students should sketch a rectangle whose dimensions are factors of the composite numbers from their rectangle in Exercise 20. Possible answers based on one dimension of 18 cm: 2 cm by 9 cm or 3 cm by 6 cm

22. $2 \cdot 3 \cdot 3 \cdot 3$ **23.** $2 \cdot 3^3$

24. These factors cannot be used to create a rectangular box because there are more than three prime factors.

25. $2 \cdot 5 \cdot 7$ **26.** $3 \cdot 19$ **27.** 2^6

28. 3^4; students should sketch a 3-cm-by-3-cm rectangle.

29. $2^3 \cdot 3 \cdot 5$; students should sketch a 2-cm-by-2-cm rectangle.

30. Check student responses.

Long-Term Project—Chapter 1

1. Check students' estimates.

2. Student responses should include the idea that the discount could become more than the cost of the cleaning service.

3. $i = 75c$ **4.** $2400 **5.** $6000 **6.** $7500

7. The amount of the monthly discount, or amount saved by each customer

8. $1.25 **9.** $18 **10.** $p = \$75 - d$

11. $73.75 **12.** $70.75 **13.** $68

14.

c	d	p	i
100	$0.00	$75.00	$7500.00
101	$0.25	$74.75	$7549.75
102	$0.50	$74.50	$7599.00
103	$0.75	$74.25	$7647.75
104	$1.00	$74.00	$7606.00
105	$1.25	$73.75	$7743.75
106	$1.50	$73.50	$7791.00
107	$1.75	$73.25	$7837.75
108	$2.00	$73.00	$7884.00
109	$2.25	$72.75	$7929.75
110	$2.50	$72.50	$7975.00
111	$2.75	$72.25	$8019.75
112	$3.00	$72.00	$8064.00
113	$3.25	$71.75	$8107.75
114	$3.50	$71.50	$8151.00
115	$3.75	$71.25	$8193.75
116	$4.00	$71.00	$8236.00
117	$4.25	$70.75	$8277.75
118	$4.50	$70.50	$8319.00
119	$4.75	$70.25	$8359.75
120	$5.00	$70.00	$8400.00
121	$5.25	$69.75	$8439.75
122	$5.50	$69.50	$8479.00
123	$5.75	$69.25	$8517.75
124	$6.00	$69.00	$8556.00

125	$6.25	$68.75	$8593.75	179	$19.75	$55.25	$9889.75
126	$6.50	$68.50	$8631.00	180	$20.00	$55.00	$9900.00
127	$6.75	$68.25	$8667.75	181	$20.25	$54.75	$9909.75
128	$7.00	$68.00	$8704.00	182	$20.50	$54.50	$9919.00
129	$7.25	$67.75	$8739.75	183	$20.75	$54.25	$9927.75
130	$7.50	$67.50	$8775.00	184	$21.00	$54.00	$9936.00
131	$7.75	$67.25	$8809.75	185	$21.25	$53.75	$9943.75
132	$8.00	$67.00	$8844.00	186	$21.50	$53.50	$9951.00
133	$8.25	$66.75	$8877.75	187	$21.75	$53.25	$9957.75
134	$8.50	$66.50	$8911.00	188	$22.00	$53.00	$9964.00
135	$8.75	$66.25	$8943.75	189	$22.25	$52.75	$9969.75
136	$9.00	$66.00	$8976.00	190	$22.50	$52.50	$9975.00
137	$9.25	$65.75	$9007.75	191	$22.75	$52.25	$9979.75
138	$9.50	$65.50	$9039.00	192	$23.00	$52.00	$9984.00
139	$9.75	$65.25	$9069.75	193	$23.25	$51.75	$9987.75
140	$10.00	$65.00	$9100.00	194	$23.50	$51.50	$9991.00
141	$10.25	$64.75	$9129.75	195	$23.75	$51.25	$9993.75
142	$10.50	$64.50	$9159.00	196	$24.00	$51.00	$9996.00
143	$10.75	$64.25	$9187.75	197	$24.25	$50.75	$9997.75
144	$11.00	$64.00	$9216.00	198	$24.50	$50.50	$9999.00
145	$11.25	$63.75	$9243.75	199	$24.75	$50.25	$9999.75
146	$11.50	$63.50	$9271.00	200	$25.00	$50.00	$10000.00
147	$11.75	$63.25	$9297.75	201	$25.25	$49.75	$9999.75
148	$12.00	$63.00	$9324.00	202	$25.50	$49.50	$9999.00
149	$12.25	$62.75	$9349.75	203	$25.75	$49.25	$9997.75
150	$12.50	$62.50	$9375.00	204	$26.00	$49.00	$9996.00
151	$12.75	$62.25	$9399.75	205	$26.25	$48.75	$9993.75
152	$13.00	$62.00	$9424.00	206	$26.50	$48.50	$9991.00
153	$13.25	$61.75	$9447.75	207	$26.75	$48.25	$9987.75
154	$13.50	$61.50	$9471.00	208	$27.00	$48.00	$9984.00
155	$13.75	$61.25	$9493.75	209	$27.25	$47.75	$9979.75
156	$14.00	$61.00	$9516.00	210	$27.50	$47.50	$9975.00
157	$14.25	$60.75	$9537.75	211	$27.75	$47.25	$9969.75
158	$14.50	$60.50	$9559.00	212	$28.00	$47.00	$9964.00
159	$14.75	$60.25	$9579.75	213	$28.25	$46.75	$9957.75
160	$15.00	$60.00	$9600.00	214	$28.50	$46.50	$9951.00
161	$15.25	$59.75	$9619.75	215	$28.75	$46.25	$9943.75
162	$15.50	$59.50	$9639.00	216	$29.00	$46.00	$9936.00
163	$15.75	$59.25	$9657.75	217	$29.25	$45.75	$9927.75
164	$16.00	$59.00	$9676.00	218	$29.50	$45.50	$9919.00
165	$16.25	$58.75	$9693.75	219	$29.75	$45.25	$9909.75
166	$16.50	$58.50	$9711.00	220	$30.00	$45.00	$9900.00
167	$16.75	$58.25	$9727.75	221	$30.25	$44.75	$9889.75
168	$17.00	$58.00	$9744.00	222	$30.50	$44.50	$9879.00
169	$17.25	$57.75	$9759.75	223	$30.75	$44.25	$9867.75
170	$17.50	$57.50	$9775.00	224	$31.00	$44.00	$9856.00
171	$17.75	$57.25	$9789.75	225	$31.25	$43.75	$9843.75
172	$18.00	$57.00	$9804.00	226	$31.50	$43.50	$9831.00
173	$18.25	$56.75	$9817.75	227	$31.75	$43.25	$9817.75
174	$18.50	$56.50	$9831.00	228	$32.00	$43.00	$9804.00
175	$18.75	$56.25	$9843.75	229	$32.25	$42.75	$9789.75
176	$19.00	$56.00	$9856.00	230	$32.50	$42.50	$9775.00
177	$19.25	$55.75	$9867.75	231	$32.75	$42.25	$9759.75
178	$19.50	$55.50	$9879.00	232	$33.00	$42.00	$9744.00

ANSWERS

233	$33.25	$41.75	$9727.75
234	$33.50	$41.50	$9711.00
235	$33.75	$41.25	$9693.75
236	$34.00	$41.00	$9676.00
237	$34.25	$40.75	$9657.75
238	$34.50	$40.50	$9639.00
239	$34.75	$40.25	$9619.75
240	$35.00	$40.00	$9600.00
241	$35.25	$39.75	$9579.75
242	$35.50	$39.50	$9559.00
243	$35.75	$39.25	$9537.75
244	$36.00	$39.00	$9516.00
245	$36.25	$38.75	$9493.75
246	$36.50	$38.50	$9471.00
247	$36.75	$38.25	$9447.75
248	$37.00	$38.00	$9424.00
249	$37.25	$37.75	$9399.75
250	$37.50	$37.50	$9375.00
251	$37.75	$37.25	$9349.75
252	$38.00	$37.00	$9324.00
253	$38.25	$36.75	$9297.75
254	$38.50	$36.50	$9271.00
255	$38.75	$36.25	$9243.75
256	$39.00	$36.00	$9216.00
257	$39.25	$35.75	$9187.75
258	$39.50	$35.50	$9159.00
259	$39.75	$35.25	$9129.75
260	$40.00	$35.00	$9100.00
261	$40.25	$34.75	$9069.75
262	$40.50	$34.50	$9039.00
263	$40.75	$34.25	$9007.75
264	$41.00	$34.00	$8976.00
265	$41.25	$33.75	$8943.75
266	$41.50	$33.50	$8911.00
267	$41.75	$33.25	$8877.75
268	$42.00	$33.00	$8844.00
269	$42.25	$32.75	$8809.75
270	$42.50	$32.50	$8775.00
271	$42.75	$32.25	$8739.75
272	$43.00	$32.00	$8704.00
273	$43.25	$31.75	$8667.75
274	$43.50	$31.50	$8631.00
275	$43.75	$31.25	$8593.75
276	$44.00	$31.00	$8556.00
277	$44.25	$30.75	$8517.75
278	$44.50	$30.50	$8479.00
279	$44.75	$30.25	$8439.75
280	$45.00	$30.00	$8400.00
281	$45.25	$29.75	$8359.75
282	$45.50	$29.50	$8319.00
283	$45.75	$29.25	$8277.75
284	$46.00	$29.00	$8236.00
285	$46.25	$28.75	$8193.75

15. 241 customers   **16.** $9375.00; $9375.00

17. 200 customers

18. Check student responses.

19. $y = 12i$ **20.** $104,013   **21.** $120,000

22. Students should give reasons for or against the use of the promotion.

Lab Activity—Chapter 2

1. -5; student sketches should show neutral pairs circled and 5 negative counters remaining.

2. 7; student sketches should show neutral pairs circled and 7 positive counters remaining.

3. -4; student sketches should show neutral pairs circled and 4 negative counters remaining.

4. 5; student sketches should show neutral pairs circled and 5 positive counters remaining.

5. Check student guidelines. Possible answer: When adding positive and negative integers, find the sum of all the positive integers. Next find the sum of all the negative integers. Subtract the absolute values of these sums. Use the sign from the number with the larger absolute value.

6. 432   **7.** 149   **8.** 1480   **9.** -1111

10. 140   **11.** -699 **12.** -6 **13.** 20

14. 30,340 feet   **15.** 20,602 feet

16. 2; student sketches should show 7 moves left and 9 moves right, ending on 2.

17. -7; student sketches should show 4 moves right and 11 moves left, ending on -7.

18. -1; student sketches should show 4 moves left, 8 moves right, and 5 moves left, ending on -1.

ANSWERS

19. 0; student sketches should show 10 moves left, 18 moves right, 3 moves left, and 5 moves left, ending on 0.

20. $1021.59; black

21. Check students' problems and answers.

Long-Term Project— Chapter 2

1. approximately 3750 miles

2. approximately 2200 miles

3. $t = \$19.95d + \$0.19m$

4. $t = \$21.50d + \$0.17m$

5. $t = \$14.95d + \$0.15m$

6. $t = \$39.99d$ 7. $t = \$41.50d$

8. no unlimited daily rate

9. $t = \$248.79 + \$19.95d + \$0.19m$

10. $t = \$225.50 + \$21.50d + \$0.17m$

11. no weekly rate

12. $t = \$248.79 + \$39.99d$

13. $t = \$225.50 + \$41.50d$

14. no weekly rate

15.
Florida	California
$930.05	$635.55
$359.91	$359.91
$644.94	$497.69
$328.77	$328.77
$865.00	$601.50
$373.50	$373.50
$587.25	$455.50
$308.50	$308.50
$727.05	$494.55
n/a	n/a
n/a	n/a
n/a	n/a

16–17. The answer for both Florida and California is Cross-Country Cars' weekly rate plus daily rate with unlimited miles, totaling $308.50.

18. a. $t = a + \$19.95d + \$0.19m$
    b. $t = a + \$39.99d$
    c. $t = a + \$248.79 + \$19.95d + \$0.19m$
    d. $t = a + \$248.79 + \$39.99d$

19. a. $t = a + \$21.50d + \$0.17m$
    b. $t = a + \$41.50d$
    c. $t = a + \$225.50 + \$21.50d + \$0.17m$
    d. $t = a + \$225.50 + \$41.50d$

20. a. $t = a + \$14.95d + \$0.15m$
    b–d. n/a

21.
Florida	California
$761.55	$623.55
$903.91	$765.91
$842.19	$704.19
$872.77	$734.77
$771.50	$633.50
$917.50	$779.50
$821.00	$683.00
$852.50	$714.50
$708.55	$570.55
n/a	n/a
n/a	n/a
n/a	n/a

22. Renting from Attractive Auto Rental at a daily rate with a charge per mile is the cheapest, totaling $708.50 with air fare.

23. Renting from Attractive Auto Rental at a daily rate with a charge per mile is the cheapest, totaling $570.55 with air fare.

24. Check student responses. Examples are driving time vs. flying time, two fewer nights in hotels if they drive through the night, and cost of gasoline.

25. Driving to California in a rental car from Cross-Country Cars at the weekly rate plus the daily rate with unlimited miles is the cheapest option. Using the same car rental option to drive to Florida seems to be equally cheap until you consider the cost of gasoline and other expenses.

Lab Activity—Chapter 3

The answers for this lab activity will depend on the number of each color of jelly beans in each student's sample. You may want to purchase a large bag of jelly beans and divide them up into small bags with a consistent number for each color in order to simplify the checking of answers for this lab activity.

Long-Term Project— Chapter 3

1. $\frac{1}{2}$ 2. $\frac{1}{6}$ 3. $\frac{1}{3}$ 4. $\frac{1}{4}$ 5. $\frac{1}{12}$ 6. $\frac{2}{3}$

7. 510 min; 170 min; 340 min

8. 255 min; 85 min; 680 min

9. 570 min; 190 min; 380 min

10. 285 min; 95 min; 760 min

11. $61\frac{1}{2}$ h; $20\frac{1}{2}$ h; 41 h;

12. $30\frac{3}{4}$ h; $10\frac{1}{4}$ h; 82 h

13. $\frac{1}{2}; \frac{1}{6}; \frac{1}{3}$ 14. $\frac{1}{4}; \frac{1}{12}; \frac{2}{3}$

15. 50%; 16.7%; 33.3%

16. 25%; 8.3%; 66.7%

17. $\frac{10}{19}; \frac{3}{19}; \frac{6}{19}$ 18. $\frac{4}{19}; \frac{2}{19}; \frac{13}{19}$

19. $\frac{2}{19}; \frac{8}{19}; \frac{3}{19}; \frac{6}{19}$

20. 4 times out of 19   21. 2 times out of 19

22. Check students' responses. Students should develop a plan that indicates the number of minutes for each light based on the conditions listed.

23–30. The answers to these exercises depend on the plan the student developed for Exercise 22.

31. Check students' responses. The student should have explained why he or she does or does not think that the plan would be acceptable.

Lab Activity—Chapter 4

Check that students construct polygons with sides of the given length(s) and angles of the given measures for Exercises 1–10.

1. 90° 2. 60° 3. 30°, 120°

4. 45° 5. 108°

6. Its sides and angles are not congruent.

7. 120° each 8. a four-sided polygon

9. 150° each 10. 120°

11. Hexagon; possible answer: it has the greatest number of sides, each 2 inches long.

12. Square and rhombus; possible answer: each has four sides that are 2 inches long.

13. regular pentagon, regular hexagon, rhombus

14. equilateral triangle

15. square and isosceles right triangle

16. isosceles triangle

17. rhombus, isosceles trapezoid

18. square

19. irregular pentagon and irregular quadrilateral

20–26. Check student responses. Students should have written lists of clues that fit the conditions and determined what polygon(s) fit their list of clues.

Long-Term Project— Chapter 4

Check student diagrams in Exercises 1–15 to see whether they illustrate the given term. Possible definitions are given here.

1. an angle measuring less than 90°

2. an angle measuring 90°

3. an angle measuring more than 90°

4. two angles whose measures have a sum of 90°

5. two angles whose measures have a sum of 180°

6. two lines that are always the same distance apart, so they never meet

7. two lines that meet at right angles

8. a line that intersects two other lines in the same plane

9. a value that represents the ratio of corresponding sides of two similar figures

10. a polygon in which a line segment connecting two points inside the polygon is not contained inside the polygon

11. a polygon in which any line segment connecting two points inside the polygon is contained inside the polygon

12. a triangle with two congruent sides

13. a triangle with three congruent sides

14. a triangle whose sides are unequal in measure

15. a polygon whose sides and angles are all congruent

16–29. Student responses will depend on their choice of item in Exercise 16. Review individual student work. Students will need to exchange information with another student to complete Exercises 22–29.

Lab Activity—Chapter 5

1. $-(x + y) = -x - y$; squares 1 and 5

2. $-x + y - y = -x$; squares 2 and 11

3. $2x - (-1) - 2x = 1$; squares 3 and 19

4. $(x + y) - (y + x) = 0$; squares 4 and 22

5. $x - (x + 1) = -1$; squares 6 and 9

6. $2x + y - x - y = x$; squares 7 and 13

7. $x + y - 2x = -x + y$; squares 8 and 10

8. $(x + 1) - (x - 1) = 2$; squares 12 and 18

9. $2(x + y) - (x + y) = x + y$; squares 14 and 17

10. $x + (y - x) = y$; squares 15 and 16

11. $2x - 3y - x + 2y = x - y$; squares 20 and 21

12. $x - (x + y) = -y$; squares 23 and 24

Long-Term Project— Chapter 5

1. The sum of each row, column, and diagonal is equal to 34.

2. The sum of the numbers in each broken diagonal is 34.

3. Yes. The array is a panmagic square because the sum of each row, column, main diagonal, and broken diagonal is equal to 34, the magic-square constant.

4.

14	7	12	1
11	2	13	8
5	16	3	10
4	9	6	15

The new array is a panmagic square.

5.

1	12	7	14
8	13	2	11
10	3	16	5
15	6	9	4

The new array is a panmagic square.

6.

▽ *a* **20**	▽ *b* **8**	▽ *c* **11**	▽ *d* **23**
▽ *e* **15**	▽ *f* **19**	▽ *g* **16**	▽ *h* **12**
▽ *i* **17**	▽ *j* **13**	▽ *k* **14**	▽ *l* **18**
▽ *m* **10**	▽ *n* **22**	▽ *o* **21**	▽ *p* **9**

7. The square is magic because the sum of the numbers in each row, column, and main diagonal is 62. It is not panmagic because the sum of the numbers in each broken diagonal is not 62.

8. The sum of each row, column, and main diagonal is $4x - 10$.

9. $(x - 6, x - 8, x + 1, x + 3)$;
$(x - 2, x - 9, x - 3, x + 4)$;
$(x - 5, x + 2, x, x - 7)$;
$(x - 4, x + 5, x - 1, x - 10)$;
$(x - 2, x - 6, x - 3, x + 1)$;
$(x - 1, x - 5, x - 4, x)$

10. The sum of each broken diagonal is $4x - 10$.

11. The sum of the expressions in each row, column, main diagonal, and broken diagonal is $4x - 10$.

12. Answers may vary. Sample answer:

$x - 7$	$x - 6$	$x + 6$	$x + 5$
$x + 4$	$x + 7$	$x - 5$	$x - 8$
$x - 1$	$x - 4$	x	$x + 3$
$x + 2$	$x + 1$	$x - 3$	$x - 2$

13–14. Answers may vary.

15. Each sum is 62.

16. Answers may vary. Sample answer:

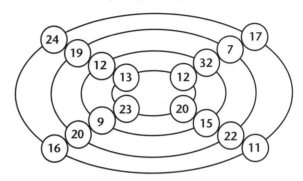

17. Answers may vary. Sample answer:

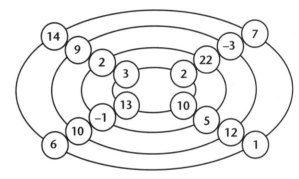

The new array is a planetarium array.

18. Answers may vary. Sample answer:

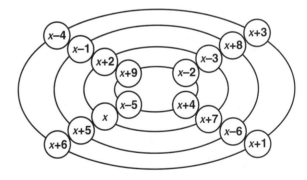

Lab Activity—Chapter 6

The order of the answers may vary.

1. Possible answer: $5x = 10$

ANSWERS

2. Possible answer: multiplication

3. The "Find the Solution" half of the viewer helps you identify the property needed to solve the equation: $x = 2$.

4.

Equation	Type
$5x = 10$	multiplication
$\frac{x}{3} = -2$	division
$-x = -2$	multiplication
$\frac{x}{12} = \frac{2}{3}$	division
$\frac{x}{0.9} = 10$	division
$\frac{1}{2}x = 4$	multiplication

Property	Solution
Division Property of Equality	$x = 2$
Multiplication Property of Equality	$x = -6$
Division Property of Equality	$x = 2$
Multiplication Property of Equality	$x = 8$
Multiplication Property of Equality	$x = 9$
Division Property of Equality	$x = 8$

5. **a.** x divided by 5 is $\frac{2}{15}$

   $\frac{2}{15}$ multiplied by 5 is $\frac{2}{3}$

   b. x multiplied by 3 is -23

   -23 divided by 3 is $-7\frac{2}{3}$

   c. x multiplied by $-\frac{1}{4}$ is -2

   -2 divided by $-\frac{1}{4}$ is 8

   d. x divided by $\frac{1}{2}$ is -1

   -1 multiplied by $\frac{1}{2}$ is $-\frac{1}{2}$

   e. 6 divided by x is $\frac{1.2}{4}$

   $\frac{4}{1.2}$ multiplied by 6 is 20

   f. x multiplied by $-\frac{1}{5}$ is 1

1 divided by $-\frac{1}{5}$ is -5

Long-Term Project—Chapter 6

1. $\dfrac{\text{Requisition}}{\text{Argument}} = \dfrac{\text{Produce}}{\text{Fruit}}$, or equivalent proportion

2. Possible answer:
   Requisition = number of items needed or desired to be purchased
   Produce = cost of purchase
   Argument = number of items sold as a group
   Fruit = total cost of items sold as a group

   (Note: Fruit divided by Argument gives the unit cost.)

3. Possible answer: He multiplied Produce (9) by Argument $\left(\frac{5}{2}\right)$ and then divided by Fruit $\left(\frac{3}{7}\right)$.

4. Possible proportion: $\dfrac{r}{\frac{5}{2}} = \dfrac{9}{\frac{3}{7}}$, where $r =$ Requisition; $r = 52\frac{1}{2}$ palas

5. Fruit = 40 libras; Argument = 100 rotuli; Requisition = 5 rotuli; Produce = 2 libras.

6. Possible answer: $\dfrac{(9)(16)(5)}{(6)(10)} = x$

7. 12 days

8. Possible answer: $\dfrac{(30)(4400)(9)}{(36)(1000)} = x$; $x = 33$ days

9. Possible answer: Let $t =$ number of days; $\dfrac{250t}{7} + \dfrac{250t}{9} = 250$; $t = \dfrac{(250)(63)}{4000}$

10. $109\frac{3}{8}$ miles

11. The sum of the distances covered by each courier must be 250 miles.

12. Both problems involve distance.

13. The cars will meet in 2 hours. The faster car travels 140 miles; the slower car travels 130 miles.

ANSWERS

Lab Activity—Chapter 7

1. **a.** Subtraction Property of Equality
   b. Group like terms and simplify.
   c. Addition Property of Equality
   d. Group like terms and simplify.
   e. Division Property of Equality

2. Substitute 10 for x into the original equation. Evaluate both sides.

3. **a.** -1;
   b. $\div -1$; $\div -1$ or $\times -1$; $\times -1$

4. **a.** $+ 2$; $+ 2$
   b. $\times 4$; $\times 4$

5. **a.** Distributive Property
   b. Subtract $5b$.
   c. Add 20.
   d. Divide by 3.

6. **a.** Subtract $2t$.
   b. Add 1.
   c. Divide by 2.
   d. Check by substituting 2 for t.

7–30.

$3b + 9 = -2b + 29$			
7 $3b + 9$	15 $+2b$	19 $+2b$	23 $-2b + 29$
8 $2b + 3b + 9$			24 $2b - 2b + 29$
9 $5b + 9$	16 $- 9$	20 $- 9$	25 29
10 $5b + 9 - 9$			26 $29 - 9$
11 $5b$	17 $\div 5$	21 $\div 5$	27 20
12 b	18 $b = 4$	22 $b = 4$	28 4
13 $3(4) + 9$			29 $-2(4) + 29$
14 21			30 21

31.

$2y + 1 = 5$			
$2y + 1$	-1	-1	5
$2y + 1 - 1$			$5 - 1$
$2y$	$\div 2$	$\div 2$	4
y	$y = 2$	$y = 2$	2
$2(2) + 1$			5
5			5

32.

$2b - 7 = -2 + b$			
$2b - 7$	$- b$	$- b$	$-2 + b$
$2b - b - 7$			$-2 + b - b$
$b - 7$	$+ 7$	$+ 7$	-2
$b - 7 + 7$			$-2 + 7$
b	$b = 5$	$b = 5$	5
$2(5) - 7$			$-2 + 5$
3			3

ANSWERS

Long-Term Project— Chapter 7

1. $\frac{1}{3}x$ 2. $x - \frac{1}{3}x$ or $\left(1 - \frac{1}{3}\right)x$ 3. $\frac{1}{4}\left(1 - \frac{1}{3}\right)x$

4. Given

5. Simplify parentheses.

6. Simplify fractions.

7. Combine like terms.

8. Multiplication Property of Equality

9. Division Property of Equality

10. Substitute 40 for x.

$$\frac{1}{3}(40) + \frac{1}{4}\left(\frac{2}{3}\right)(40) + \frac{1}{5}\left(\frac{3}{4}\right)\left(\frac{2}{3}\right)(40) \stackrel{?}{=} 24$$

$$\frac{40}{3} + \frac{20}{3} + 4 \stackrel{?}{=} 24$$

$$\frac{60}{3} + 4 \stackrel{?}{=} 24$$

$$20 + 4 \stackrel{?}{=} 24$$

$$24 = 24$$

11. $\frac{1}{6}x + \frac{1}{5}\left(\frac{5}{6}\right)x + \frac{1}{4}\left(\frac{4}{5}\right)\left(\frac{5}{6}\right)x + \frac{1}{3}\left(\frac{3}{4}\right)\left(\frac{4}{5}\right)\left(\frac{5}{6}\right)x +$

$\frac{1}{2}\left(\frac{2}{3}\right)\left(\frac{3}{4}\right)\left(\frac{4}{5}\right)\left(\frac{5}{6}\right)x + 3 = x$

12. There were 18 mangoes in the collection.

13. $\frac{5}{6}(18) + 3 \stackrel{?}{=} 18$

$$15 + 3 \stackrel{?}{=} 18$$

$$18 = 18$$

14. $1 + \frac{1}{2}x + 1 + \frac{1}{4}x + \frac{1}{2} + \frac{1}{8}x + \frac{1}{4} + \frac{1}{16} +$

$\frac{1}{8} + \frac{1}{32}x + \frac{1}{16} + \frac{1}{64}x + \frac{1}{32} + \frac{1}{128}x + \frac{1}{64} = x$

15. $\frac{127}{128}x + \frac{191}{64} = x$ 16. $\frac{191}{64} = \frac{1}{128}x$

17. $382 = x$

18. $\frac{1}{2}x + \frac{1}{8}x + \frac{1}{10}x + \frac{1}{20}x + \frac{1}{60}x + 50 = x$

19. $240 = x$

20. Students' check should begin with the following:

$$\frac{1}{2}(240) + \frac{1}{8}(240) + \frac{1}{10}(240) + \frac{1}{20}(240) +$$

$$\frac{1}{60}(24) + 50 \stackrel{?}{=} 240$$

21. 90 hours

Lab Activity—Chapter 8

1. by rubber bands stretched across the vertical and horizontal axes

2. at the center peg enclosed by both rubber bands

3. 1   4. 1

5. When two different pairs of points are on the same line, the slopes of the lines they represent are the same.

6. 1

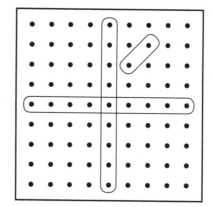

7. 1

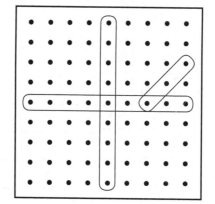

8. 1

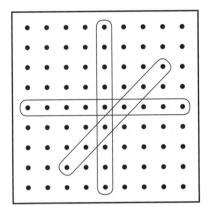

9. $\frac{1}{2}$

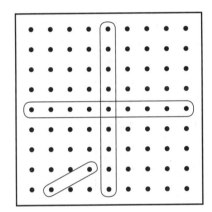

10. −1

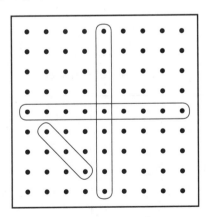

11. 4

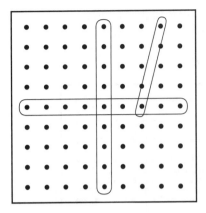

12.

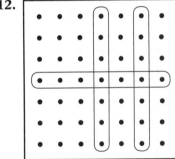

6

13. 0   **14.** undefined

15. slope $= \frac{3 - (-3)}{2 - 2} = \frac{6}{0}$; division by zero is undefined, so the line has no slope.

16.

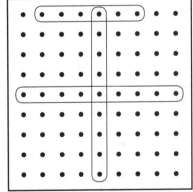

0

17. 5   **18.** 0

ANSWERS

19. slope = $\dfrac{4-4}{-3-2} = \dfrac{0}{-5} = 0$; the two points on the horizontal line have the same y-coordinate. The change in y is 0.

20. Answers will vary. Possible answer:

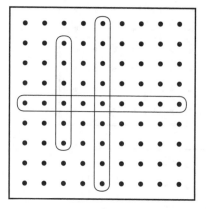

$(-2, 3)$, $(-2, -2)$

21. Answers will vary. Possible answer:

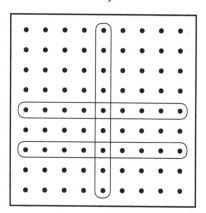

$(-4, -2)$, $(4, -2)$

22. Answers will vary. Possible answer:

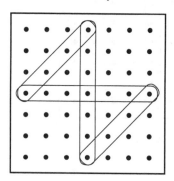

23. 1; 1; they are equal.

24. Answers will vary. Possible answer:

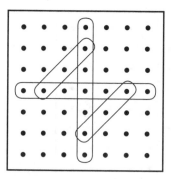

25. Answers will vary; 1 and 1 for the sample answer.

26. Parallel lines have the same slope.

27. Answers will vary. Possible answer:

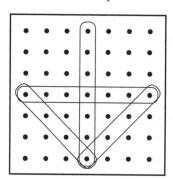

28. Answers will vary; -1 and 1 for the sample answer.

29. -1

30. Answers will vary. Possible answer:

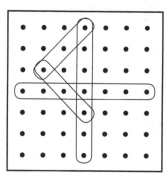

31. Answers will vary; -1 and 1 for the sample answer

32. -1

HRW Algebra One Interactions Course 1

ANSWERS

33. Two lines are perpendicular if the product of their slopes is -1. The slopes of perpendicular lines are negative reciprocals of one another.

Long-Term Project—Chapter 8

1. $(5, 1), (5, 8)$

2. $(-9, -9), (-3, -9), (-9, -7), (-3, -7)$

3. $(5, -7), (8, -4), (4, -6), (7, -3)$

Lab Activity—Chapter 9

1.

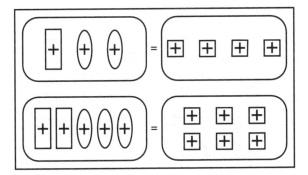

2. Subtract $2y$ from each side of the equation; $x = -2y + 4$

3.

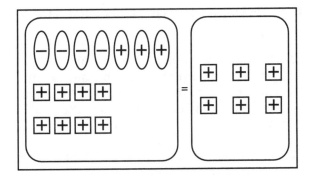

4.

5. Combine like terms, subtract 8 from each side of the equation, and then multiply each side by -1; $y = 2$

6.

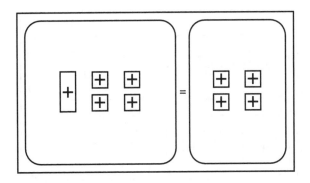

7. Subtract 4 from each side of the equation; $x = 0$

8. Substitute the values for x and y into the original equations.

9. $x = 6, y = 1$

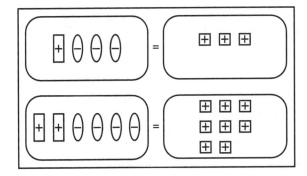

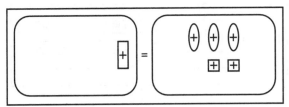

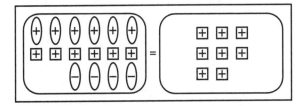

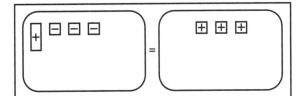

10.

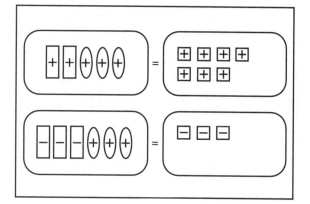

16. $x = -4, y = -1$

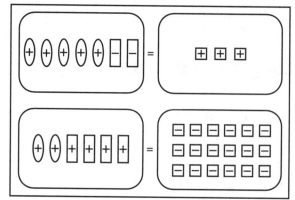

11. -1

12–13.

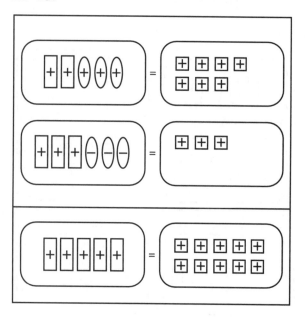

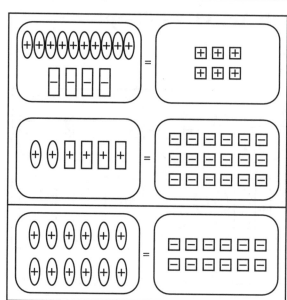

17. Check students' responses. Students should create original problems, sketch the solution steps, and record the correct answers to the problems.

Long-Term Project—Chapter 9

1. Student descriptions should include graphing the equations on the same set of axes and using the coordinates of the point of intersection as the solution to the system.

2. Student descriptions should include solving one of the equations for one variable and then substituting for that variable in the other equation.

14. $x = 2$ **15.** $y = 1$

ANSWERS

3. Student descriptions should include adding or subtracting the equations to form a pair of opposites, thus eliminating one of the variables.

4. Student descriptions should include multiplying one or both equations to form a pair of opposites and then using addition to eliminate one of the variables.

5. $17,500c + 22,300t = 1,855,600$

6. $c + t = 100$ **7.** cars = 78; trucks = 22

8. Student methods may vary. Possible answer: Use substitution because it's easy to solve for c or t in the second equation.

9. $m + c = 100$

10. $26,400m + 17,500c = 1,972,500$

11. minivans = 25; other cars = 75

12. Student methods may vary. Possible answer: Multiply the first equation by $-26,400$, and then add to eliminate m.

13. 3 cars **14.** $2,463,100 **15.** $557,500

16. $21,400s + 23,650b = 557,500$

17. $s + b = 25$

18. small trucks = 15; big trucks = 10

19. Student methods may vary. Possible answer: Solve each equation for s, and then use a graphics calculator to graph the equations and to find the point of intersection.

20. $e + s = 75$; $16,400e + 21,900s = 1,312,500$

21. economy cars = 60; sports cars = 15

22. Student methods may vary. Possible answer: Use substitution because it's easy to solve for e or s in the first equation.

23–25. Check student responses. Students should design their own car lots by using systems of equations to determine prices and numbers of vehicles. Their work should include a description of how systems of equations were used.

Lab Activity—Chapter 10

1. Area of region II = 1 square unit
Area of region III = 2.5 square units
Thus, the area of the polygon is 1.5 + 1 + 2.5 = 5 square units.

2.

Boundary dots	3	4	5	6	7
Area	0.5	1	1.5	2	2.5

3. 4.5 square units; answers will vary. Possible answers:

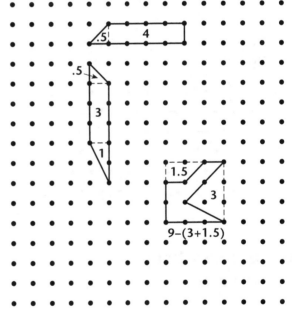

4. $A(n) = \frac{n}{2} - 1$

5.

Boundary dots	4	5	6	7	8
Area	2	2.5	3	3.5	4

---

6. 6 square units. Answers will vary. Possible answers:

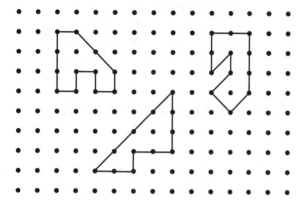

7. $A(n) = \frac{n}{2}$

8. The new rule is one unit larger for every n.

9.

Boundary dots	3	4	5	6	7
Area	1	2	3	4	5

10. $A(n) = n - 2$

11. 7 square units; answers will vary; possible answer:

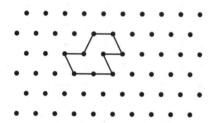

Long-Term Project— Chapter 10

1. $1061.36 **2.** $1082.86 **3.** $1131.41

4. $1085.79 **5.** $1156.82 **6.** $1108.72

7. $1176.26 **8.** $1240.41

9.

Principal	Rate	Number of interest periods per year
$1000	3%	2
$1000	4%	4
$1000	5%	2
$1000	5.5%	12
$1000	6%	1
$1000	7%	2
$1000	8.2%	4
$1000	9%	1

Time	Amount in account	Interest earned
2	$1,061.36	$ 61.36
2	$1,082.86	$ 82.86
2	$1,103.81	$103.81
2	$1,116.00	$116.00
2	$1,123.60	$123.60
2	$1,147.52	$147.52
2	$1,176.26	$176.26
2	$1,188.10	$188.10

10. Answers will vary.

11. Answers will vary.

12. Answers will vary.

13–16. Check students' graphs.

17. Answers will vary. Possible answer: Fixed rental car rates with no additional charges for extra mileage will be represented by linear functions.

18. Answers will vary. Possible answer: Fixed rental car rates up to a specific number of miles with extra charges for additional miles will be represented by non-constant linear functions.

19. Answers will vary.

Lab Activity—Chapter 11

1–27. Check students' work. Answers will vary according to data collected.

ANSWERS

28. Answers may vary. Possible answers: A teacher would then know how much time to allow for reading. He or she may also gain some information about the reading abilities of the students.

Long-Term Project—Chapter 11

1. 22

2. Find the sum of the numbers, and divide by 20.

3. 22

4. List the totals in numerical order, and find the middle value.

5. 19, 21, 22, 23, 26

6. Find the values that are listed the most often.

7. 8

8. Subtract the smallest total from the largest total.

9.

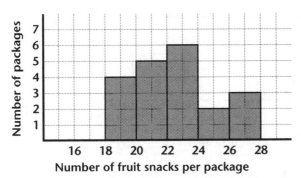

10. LQ = 20; UQ = 23.5

11.

12. purple = 3   **13.** green = 3

14. yellow = 4   **15.** blue = 6   **16.** red = 4

17. orange = 2   **18.** 22   **19.** purple = 14%

20. green = 14%   **21.** yellow = 18%

22. blue = 27%   **23.** red = 18%

24. orange = 9%

25.

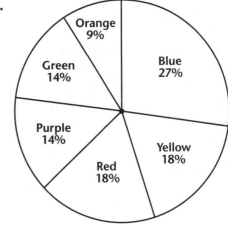

26. purple = 42   **27.** green = 42

28. yellow = 54   **29.** blue = 81

30. red = 54   **31.** orange = 27

32. yellow and red   **33.** 4   **34.** 6

35. Students should describe in detail a situation for which they could conduct a similar statistical study.

Lab Activity—Chapter 12

1. Answers may vary.

2. Answers may vary. Students' answers should indicate that they multiplied the length of the diameter by π to find the circumference.

3. Answers may vary. Students' answers should indicate that they multiplied the square of the radius by π to find the area.

4. rectangle

ANSWERS

5. Answers may vary. Students' answers should indicate that they multiplied the length of the rectangle (the circumference of the circle) by the width of the rectangle (the height of the cylinder).

6. Answers may vary. Students should find the sum of twice the area of the base that they found in Exercise 3 and the area of the rectangle that they found in Exercise 5.

7. sector of a circle

8. Answers may vary. Students' answers should indicate that they multiplied the radius of the sector (the slant height of the cone) by $\frac{1}{2}$ of the length of the arc (the circumference of the circular base) to find the area of the shape.

9. Answers may vary.

10–11. Answers may vary.

12. The volume of the cone is $\frac{1}{3}$ of the volume of the cylinder.

13. $V = \frac{1}{3}\pi r^2 h$

14. Answers may vary.

15. Answers may vary. Students' answers should indicate that they multiplied the length of one side by 4 to find the perimeter of the base.

16. Answers may vary. Students' answers should indicate that they squared the length of the side to find the area.

17. square

18. Answers may vary.

19. isosceles triangle

20. Answers may vary. Students' answers should indicate that they multiplied the base of the triangle by $\frac{1}{2}$ of the length from the vertex to the center of the base (the slant height of the pyramid) to find the area.

21. Answers may vary.

22–23. Answers may vary.

24. The volume of the pyramid is $\frac{1}{3}$ of the volume of the cube.

25. $V = \frac{1}{3}s^3$

26. Students' answers should indicate the same diameter as in Exercise 1 and the radius should be $\frac{1}{2}$ of the diameter.

27. Answers may vary.

28. 2

29. ≈ 14.14 cubic inches

30. 100 square feet

Long-Term Project— Chapter 12

1.

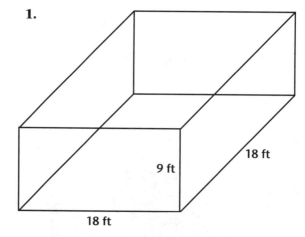

2. 729 cubic feet   3. 2916 cubic feet

4. 108 scoops   5. 1620 cubic feet

6. 60 scoops

7.

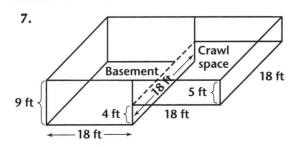

8. 4536 cubic feet   **9.** 14 loads

10. 1476 square feet   **11.** 648 square feet

12. basement: 17.5 ft by 17 ft by 8.5 ft
crawl space: 17.5 ft by 17 ft by 4.5 ft

13. 2528.75 cubic feet

14. 1338.75 cubic feet   **15.** 35.3 cubic feet

16. 54.2 square feet   **17.** 3.9 cubic feet

18. 31.4 cubic feet   **19.** 6.3 square feet

20. 42.4 cubic feet   **21.** 63.6 square feet

22. 4.7 cubic feet   **23.** 37.7 cubic feet

24. 754.0 cubic feet   **25.** 207,345.1 cubic feet

26. 12,440,706.9 cubic feet

27. 2,488,455.5 square feet

28. 34,557.5 cubic feet